JOYFUL

JOYFUL

A Truthful Guide to Finding Peace and Living a Fulfilling Life

Toks Adebiyi

ISBN: 1523335114
ISBN 13: 9781523335114
Library of Congress Control Number: 2016900561
CreateSpace Independent Publishing Platform
North Charleston, South Carolina

I dedicate this book to my wonderful mother, Olufunmilayo Olufolake Adebiyi. You taught me many life lessons I ignored as a child but have returned to as an adult. Many of your lessons were nonverbal, and although you may appear timid and fragile in public, you are indeed the strongest woman I know. Thanks a lot, my good mother; *ese gan iya mi atata*.

Contents

Acknowledgments

I must start by recognizing and honoring my Father in heaven for His guidance and wisdom, without which this book would not have come to fruition. Although I have a strong passion to help people live more fulfilling lives, I am also aware of my many limitations. Therefore, I sought His guidance every single day before writing the words in this book. He wrote the best-selling book of all time, the Bible. I thank my wife, Abi, for encouraging me to write this book. She would always ask, "Toks, how is your book going?" She was also my most important book reviewer. Thank you, Abi, for the positive pressure you put on me to make this happen. You are a great wife, and my life certainly wouldn't be as joyful without you. I thank Bimbo Dare, a good and established author; Pastor Rupert Lazar; and Dr. Cornelius Alalade, my uncle, for taking time out of their very busy schedules to provide constructive criticism, which helped in shaping the final book.

Introduction

I dreamed of writing this book for many years before I actually sat down to write it. Over the years I have experienced and witnessed others among my family, friends, and acquaintances go through life trying to appease others within society. I was in denial about this for many years and felt I was chasing my dreams, but after some intense soul-searching, I asked myself, *Why am I doing all this? What is it all for, and why is it so important to me? And why is it that whenever I achieve any of my goals, the joy is short-lived, and I soon feel a bit empty and unfulfilled?*

I would have conversations with family, friends, and colleagues, and I discovered that most people were in the same boat: living their daily lives trapped in a routine that never really brought them lasting joy or a sense of fulfilment. Most of them would talk about things they wished they could do and were truly passionate about, but they just could not break out of the routine because they were afraid of failure and of not being able to provide for those who depended on them. Even those who were able to chase their dreams still felt a sense that something was missing. What were the missing steps to lasting peace and joy?

To be honest, I had similar fears, but somehow I knew I had to change my path; it was like something within me kept me up at night telling me I was on the wrong course in life and that if I did nothing to change, I would end up with severe regrets at the end of my time on earth. I am not a writer by profession nor a motivational speaker nor a millionaire at the time of writing this book. I am an ordinary man who has made many mistakes due to a misguided understanding of what it means to be joyful. I thought having lots of money equaled success, and in my mind money was a lot more valuable than it really is. I felt that if I were really rich, my family would be happy, society would accept and respect me, and my self-confidence would be healthier. Only then would I be able to make a positive impact on the world. This false perception was the foundation of many bad decisions in which I focused on the wrong things and was often upset and frustrated when things didn't go my way. This approach made me self-centered. But thanks to taking certain steps, I am now a changed man with a very different approach to life. I am blessed with a beautiful wife and a beautiful daughter, and I have reached a state of joyfulness that cannot be bought for any price. Of course, I still encounter challenges—although most of them are consequences of bad business decisions that I made before I changed my approach. However, in general I believe that my life is now moving in the right direction—and I have a strong, ongoing faith that it will continue to do so. It is my hope that the information I am about to impart will help anyone who wishes to find that better direction in life or to stay the course.

How to Use This Book

Do you consider yourself successful, or are you barely getting by in life? Are you financially rich or poor? Are you in good or bad health? Are you happy or unhappy with your life to date? The lessons you are about to learn in this book will either totally transform your approach to life or complement it to ensure your life is worth living.

In order to get the most out of this book, I suggest you keep a notebook (or the like) handy to jot down ideas and responses as you go along. The book contains ideas and suggestions to develop a certain attitude and lifestyle that will enhance your life. You can experience this firsthand if you read the chapters in order and complete the exercises at the end of each one. Working as you go will also help to make the material more manageable.

This book teaches a better way of life based on solid principles. It teaches a balanced approach to making every day of your life count for something good, something positive, and something you will feel good about. I am convinced that if you implement the lessons in this book and do not depart from them, you will live a fulfilling life. You will achieve success in life including the following:

- You will enjoy good health.
- You will enjoy a life of peace.
- You will have a respectable and healthy family.
- You will make a positive impact on society.

- You will help many others in achieving their goals.
- You will feel fulfilled.
- You will be wealthy.
- You will be a good role model.

The ideas in this book were not developed solely by me; they have been around since the beginning of time and are timeless. What this book does is to provide context, personal stories, and examples to bring them all together in a powerful way that makes the lessons easy to understand and implement. Living a joyful life goes beyond acquiring and doing the things that give us momentary happiness; it is a combination of such things in moderation, plus loving and receiving love. This eventually leads to a healthy state of mind and inner contentment. I hope by the end of this book, you will be a better man or woman. God bless.

PS: If you are the only person who reads this book and it helps improve your life, then it will have been worth all the effort.

The Meaning of "Joyfulness"

I have studied the subject of joy for many years and can honestly say that it is a word that is very difficult to define in totality. Why? Well, because joy is actually an inner state of our being. It is something good we feel inside of us; it is an inner peace and sense of confidence or safety; it is what gets you up in the morning with a smile to face the coming day; it is faith that everything is going to work out.

You simply know it when you have joy inside of you, but you will often find it hard to describe it in words. Others will also see the joy in you, as it is evident in your expressions, words, behavior, and outlook on life. It affects you in every way; it is who you are. The dictionary describes *joyfulness* as "a state of the heart being full of joy, glad, or delighted." Here are some other great definitions of *joy*:

Joy is not in things; joy is in us.

—Benjamin Franklin

Joy is a state of mind and an orientation of the heart. It is a settled state of contentment, confidence, and hope. It is something or someone that provides a source of happiness.

—Theopedia.com

Joy is the soul of happiness. Like pleasure, it can express itself through the body, but it is not of the body. Like satisfaction, it can be felt emotionally and appreciated mentally, but it is so much more than just an emotion or a state of mind.

—DR. ROBERT HOLDEN, AUTHOR OF SEVERAL BOOKS ON HAPPINESS

Dr. Robert Holden did some great work in researching and describing the qualities of joy in an article on his blog, "Five Qualities of Joyful People." I am grateful to Robert for personally giving me permission to share these with you below.

1. **Joy is constant.**
   When people tune in to the feeling of joy, what often emerges is an awareness that this joy is somehow always with us. Joy is quietly, invisibly ever present. It is not "out there," and it is not "in here"; rather, it is simply everywhere we are. Joy feels somehow beyond space and time. Joy does not come and go; what comes and goes is our awareness of joy. Ironically, we often feel the presence of joy the most when we stop chasing pleasure and we stop trying to satisfy our ego.

2. **Joy inspires creativity.**
   Upon discovering this joy, many people experience a greater sense of creativity that rushes through them. Your ego may get the byline, but really joy is the author. Joy is the doer. Joy is the thinker. Joy is the creative principle. In one of my favorite Upanishads, classic sacred texts of Hindu literature, it is written: "From joy springs all creation, / By joy it is sustained. / Toward joy it proceeds, / and to joy it returns."

3. **Joy is often unreasonable.**
   I like to describe joy as "unreasonable happiness" because it doesn't seem to need a reason. It is a happiness that is based on nothing. In

other words, it doesn't need a cause or an effect in order to exist. Certainly good things, favorable circumstances, and a happy state of mind can make you more receptive to joy, but joy still exists even when you are not receptive to it. Joy needs no reason. And this is why we can be surprised by joy even in the most ordinary moments.

4. **Joy is untroubled.**

Unlike pleasure and satisfaction, joy does not have an opposite. It does not swing up and down as our moods do. And it does not wrestle with positives and negatives as our mind does. Joy does, however, have a twin. If pleasure's twin is pain, and satisfaction's twin is dissatisfaction, then joy's twin is love. When people describe joy to me, they always mention love—even the lawyers, the politicians, and the psychologists. Like love, joy is fearless and untroubled by the world. It is as if nothing in the world can tarnish or diminish the essence of joy. As such, it is free.

5. **Joy is enough.**

Many people describe a sense of emptiness and a "fall from grace" that follows an encounter with great pleasure and satisfaction. This is not the case with joy, however. One of the most beautiful qualities of joy is the abiding sense of "enoughness." Unlike the ephemeral states of pleasure and satisfaction, joy does not induce a craving for more, because joy is enough. If ever we feel joy is missing, it is because we are absent-minded—caught up, probably, in some grief over a passing pleasure or preoccupied with a new object of desire.

Part 1: My Story

Early Years in Sagamu

I was born in London while my mum was attending a course in industrial medicine, but I spent the first seventeen years of my life in the predominantly Christian south of Nigeria. I was born fourth of five children in my family, with two brothers and two sisters. We were raised as Christians. My mother was a medical doctor in Lagos for a government organization called the Nigerian National Petroleum Corporation (NNPC), and my father was an engineer and entrepreneur. He owned a small hotel in Ijebu Ode called Three A's Hotel, because his initials were AAA. (Ijebu Ode is the second-largest city in Ogun State after Abeokuta.)

I spent the first few years of my life, between nursery and primary school year two, in Sagamu, a limestone-rich city in Ogun in southwestern Nigeria. At the time my father worked as an engineer for West African Portland Cement (WAPCO), and we lived in an affluent housing estate of detached homes that WAPCO owned and provided for its senior staff members. Although I lived in Sagamu for a few years, I was quite young and did not really experience much of the city. This is partly because the housing estate provided everything a community needed, including a country club with squash, tennis, and swimming; children's playgrounds; community social events; and a very good nursery and primary school. So there was really no reason to leave. All I remember was that each time we left the estate, I noticed a lot of poverty in the city and could not wait to return home.

Life was very good in Sagamu, but my dad suddenly had to leave his job at WAPCO, and we had to leave the housing estate. This was a sad time for me because all my friends lived there, but my mum did a great job of selling us on our move to the prominent city of Lagos. At the time I viewed Lagos as the promised land because of all the stories I had heard about it. All my relatives that I admired and considered cool lived there in big houses, and they seemed to be much more sophisticated than we were. So I bought into the idea that we were moving up in the world, and I became excited.

Welcome to Mushin

We arrived in Lagos State—previously called and commonly referred to as Eko, the social and economic center of Nigeria—in 1988, when I was five years old. I would go on to spend the next twelve years of my life there. Like Ogun, Lagos State is also located in the southwestern part of Nigeria. It is approximately sixty-seven kilometers (about forty-two miles) from Sagamu. My mum built a two-story apartment block of four modest two-bedroom flats in Mushin, an area in Lagos that had a bad reputation because of high crime rates, poor education, inadequate sanitation, and low-quality housing. On arriving, I remember looking out the window and wondering, *What kind of place is this?* There were children running around the streets in their underwear, the roads were very bad, there was so much noise, and it generally looked like a slum. This was not what I had been expecting in Lagos. I thought everywhere would be beautiful and modern.

We arrived at our property, and although it was not nearly as good as our detached home in Sagamu, it was the best on the street. We occupied two of the adjoining flats on the top floor and rented out the two on the lower level. Things had gotten really bad for our parents, and this led to a sharp decline in our living standards, which we were not used to. It was the birth of a strong desire in me to be rich, because we were now poor. Although we probably had it better than most on our street, life in Mushin felt very hard. There was a significant drop in the quality of everything: the food we ate, the clothes we wore, the places we went. Everything felt poor when compared to our previous lives, but I took solace in knowing that we had it better than our neighbors did. They looked up to us as though we were rich.

My mum enrolled my baby sister and me into a good school called the University of Lagos Staff School (UNILAG). This was where I really noticed how poor we had become. I was no longer comforted by feelings of being better than my neighbors; now I was in a school with many rich and middle-class children. My classmates would make fun of me when I told them I lived in Mushin, so I began to cover it up, and sometimes I simply lied about where I lived. My siblings were going through similar issues. It felt horrible that I could not fit in with the cooler kids at school unless I had more lunch money, a better schoolbag, and better shoes. I needed to have visited better play areas, and most of all I needed to move out of Mushin. We simply could not afford any of these things, though, and my poor mum suffered most from the pressure we put on her. But this was now our life, and I had to accept it and live with it. So I did.

It was one of the happiest moments of my childhood when, after approximately a year, we were able to move out of Mushin. I would finally have an address I was not ashamed of. I would finally be able to mingle with the cool kids.

While we lived in Mushin, my dad would shuttle between Lagos and his hotel in Ijebu Ode each week. He would come home on Fridays and leave for work on Sundays. My relationship with my father was a bit distant; we hardly talked, and even as I write this book, our relationship is not ideal, but it is getting better. I felt my relationship with my dad was the worst of all my siblings. Sometimes I would wonder why my relationship with him was not as I hoped. Perhaps it was partly because he was often away in Ijebu Ode, or because I was so close to my mum (yes, I was a mama's boy), or maybe he just did not understand me. After all, I was an extremely shy kid who was commonly misunderstood. I had a permanent smile, which I sometimes refer to as a handicap because I could not seem to get rid of it even when I was upset or sad. When I got into trouble with my dad or anyone else, I often had a smile on my face, even though I was sorry on the inside. This led many to believe I was laughing at them or not remorseful. I suspect my dad also felt this way on such occasions.

My siblings and I did learn a lot from my dad, though. Growing up, I do not remember ever seeing him drink alcohol, and I suspect this is the reason my siblings and I hardly drink today. It is not due to our spiritual beliefs, nor do we believe there is something morally wrong with drinking alcohol; it's simply because we never acquired the taste while growing up. To me, alcohol tastes horrible, and I cannot understand why anyone enjoys beer, wine, champagne, or any drink with strong alcoholic content. (My wife, on the other hand, would strongly disagree with me.)

Another important attribute we acquired from Dad is our entrepreneurial spirit. Growing up with a father who was very business minded certainly made an impact, because all five of us have started and maintain businesses of some sort. My mum, on the other hand, was a committed and diligent employee of NNPC's private medical department for as long as I can remember until her retirement, so from a career perspective, we got to learn from both an employee and employer point of view.

The Island

We left Mushin and spent a few years living between Ebute Metta and Surulere, both suburbs in Lagos State. Then we moved to an affluent part of Lagos commonly referred to as "the Island." The Island consists of Victoria Island, Ikoyi, and Lekki peninsula. My mum had received a promotion at work and now qualified for a better official home that was owned by her employer, NNPC. It was common in those days for large organizations to provide homes for their staff as a way of retaining and rewarding them. Of course, if you left the company, you had to hand back the keys too. My mum was allocated a semidetached duplex in Dolphin Estate, Ikoyi, where I would spend the rest of my years in Lagos before relocating to the United Kingdom. The society on the Island was quite flamboyant, and although most people in Lagos were either very rich or very poor, the Island had the largest cluster of super-rich individuals in Nigeria—probably even on the African continent. On the Island the rich regularly had a good time oppressing the poor and middle class by showing off their wealth and treating people as second-class citizens. They also created an aura of exclusivity with private clubs, parties, and other social and business functions where you would only be accepted if you were one of them. Many tried to fake it but were later found out when they could not keep up with the lavish lifestyles of those they copied.

I suspect things have not changed much because, even after moving to London, I traveled back to Lagos almost every year to visit family, and on one such occasion, a wealthy friend asked me to accompany him to an exclusive nightclub. At first I thought of refusing because I really was not in the mood or interested in nightclubs at that point in my life. However, to honor his invitation, I agreed to go along on the condition that I would drive in a separate car so I could leave at my convenience. I decided to drive one of my mum's old cars because it was the only one that was readily available. I could

have taken a better car if I had waited for my sister to return, but I felt there was no need to. We drove to the nightclub in a convoy, and when we arrived, the security guards opened up the gates for us. My friend drove in with his shiny, new four-by-four, and the guards greeted him with respect. As I approached next in my mum's old car, the guards suddenly began to close the gate. They took one look at the car I was driving and demanded that I park outside on the street. It took my friend's intervention before they allowed me to park on the premises.

Feeling humiliated, I swallowed my pride and drove into the venue. All of a sudden, I noticed how bad my mum's car looked compared to how shiny and new all the other parked cars were. I can honestly say mine was the worst car on the premises by a mile. As if that was not bad enough, the nightclub had a very good view of the parking lot, and many people were chatting outside, so I thought everyone would notice the old car I had come in. My level of confidence dropped and evolved into a feeling of inadequacy. That was all it took to ruin my evening and make me think to myself that I needed to be rich someday.

As much as I loved Lagos, I have to admit that the environment in certain areas created a lot of pressure to keep up with the Joneses. Many times people were treated with disrespect if they were not rich. If you were perceived to be poor, you were the one who was likely to get sent on errands; you were the one who stood in line watching others pass by; you were the one told to leave your seat at a wedding ceremony to take a seat at the back of the hall. This made people very sensitive and put

them on the offensive against all appearances of disrespect, even when comments were sincere, and over the years it led to a kind of pride that is best described with the question "Do you know who I am?" Because of this dynamic, you would commonly hear comments such as "How dare you talk to me like that? Do you know who I am? Who is your father?"

This is one of the reasons poor and middle-class families would buy things they could not afford. They thought that if they copied the lifestyle of the wealthy, they themselves would be perceived as rich. They wanted to fit in, they wanted to be important, and they wanted to be respected.

The deepest urge in human nature is the desire to be important.

—John Dewey

Because I did not come from a rich family, I too experienced the oppression regularly and was always trying to fit in. I would visit the local markets to buy secondhand designer clothes and pretend I'd had them for a while, just to make an impression. I was living my life to win the respect of others.

While living on the Island, I attended a state-sponsored, all-boys secondary school (high school) called Kings College (KC) Lagos. It was arguably the best state-sponsored school, but it was not nearly as great as it had been during its glory days. I had begged and begged my mum to send me to KC because many of the coolest kids went there. The school was densely populated and had students from both the poorest and richest parts of society. It was also quite diverse from a cultural perspective. Because it was located in a Yoruba state (Yoruba is an ethnic group), there were many Hausas (mostly from the northern part of Nigeria) and Igbos (mostly from southeastern Nigeria). Kings College was a very tough school, and sometimes it felt like the Wild West. To achieve a reputation of social importance, you generally had to fall into one of three categories or a combination of them:

1. **Hard guys:** These were the boys who were popular with the girls and generally cool. Everyone wanted to be like them.
2. **Rackers:** These were the tough guys you didn't want to mess with. Many of them were bullies, too old for the class or simply blessed with a superior physique.
3. **Hit men or bucks'd up:** These were the boys who either came from super-rich families or those who regularly stole cash from their parents. Whatever the situation, they would usually have access to large amounts of cash.

We also had a category of boys known as "razzos," and you really did not want to be in this group. These were the wannabe hard guys who just were not cool enough, the boys who would go to parties and get thrown out. They were the boys who would have parties that no one came to except other razzos.

I started out in Kings College as a razzo. This was when I got the nickname "Showkey," after a popular musician from Ajegunle, one of the most deprived parts of Lagos. However, I did all I could to break out of this group, and I finally succeeded in my latter years at the school. My nickname then evolved from "Showkey" to "Showcaire" and "the Locaire."

You see, although my primary motivation at school should have been to learn and develop academically, it wasn't. My mother did all she could with a full-time job and five children to look after. She even got me a private tutor because I was struggling with my education, but my dream was to be the hardest guy in the school. I wanted to be socially important among the other kids, to be great. My education was secondary.

At secondary school, traveling to the United States or United Kingdom for summer vacations was a reputation-boosting phenomenon. At times it seemed that all you had to do to fit in with the cool kids and be noticed by the girls was to travel abroad. A relative of mine, who at the time had never traveled, even went so far as to study a map of London's West End so he could participate in conversations. I would listen to him tell others how to get to specific stores on Oxford Street in London, and I thought, *Wow, this guy hasn't set foot in the United Kingdom; how the heck does he know how to get there?* He would wink at me, and I kept quiet so as not to expose him.

The pressure was so great that even the rich felt pressure to outdo one another in order to remain relevant. I remember a popular girl who was very well-off but still felt the need to lie about having traveled internationally for the summer, even though she had been staying in another part of Nigeria. Back then, any time you received an international call, the phone would beep first when you picked up. When the girl called anyone in Nigeria that summer, she would push a button on the phone to create a beep, which was obviously fake because it lasted too long, was too loud, and was generally a different sound altogether. Of course she was found out, and her reputation tanked.

For most of my teenage years, I acted like someone else to stay relevant and keep up with the Joneses. If the cool rich kids traveled to London for the summer, I wanted to travel to London for the summer; if the cool rich kids carried a certain schoolbag, I wanted the same schoolbag, and so on. I based my relevance and happiness on copying those who I felt were more fortunate than I. Of course, I was never truly satisfied because it turned out to be an endless pursuit of happiness. Each time I struggled to finally acquire that schoolbag, the rich kids had moved on to an even cooler schoolbag, so I was constantly playing catch-up while suffering on the inside. I barely scraped by, and I graduated from secondary school with poor grades. Meanwhile, most of the cool kids I was trying to imitate ended up traveling to the United Kingdom and United States to further their studies. I would not see many of them often or ever again.

The Promised Land

I moved to London on January 5, 2000, to further my education at university, and although I had matured a bit more, I was still in the same frame of mind in my new environment. I found life in London to be very tough—a stern reality check. Seeing as I had only been there as a baby, I had no memory of it. All I knew and expected was what I had been told by friends who had visited the city on summer vacation. They painted a picture of heaven on earth, but I was about to find out the truth.

Most of my classmates who were in the United Kingdom to study lived on their university's campus. But my mum could not afford the accommodation fees, so I had to stay with a relative in a council estate in Kidbrooke, southeast London. It was one of the largest and most deprived council housing developments in London at the time. I stayed there for some months and left after a few incidents at the property. The exchange rate between the British pound and the Nigerian naira was very poor, so it was very expensive for my mum to send me her limited funds, and I now needed to work to earn a living. My first real job in London was as a janitor of a council estate in the Tower Hamlets. I will never forget my first day on the job, when I was required to mop all the stairs of a very tall building. I looked at my supervisor, thinking, *Is she serious?* Then she handed me the mop and said, "Get on with it."

This was a far cry from the comfort of my home in Ikoyi, Lagos. We might not have been rich, but at least I had not had to work in what I felt was such a menial and demeaning job. What if my friends found out what I was doing? My reputation would be finished.

I did this job for a while and moved on to live with a friend who was much older than I in a two-bedroom apartment in East Dulwich, southeast London, where I paid my half of the monthly rent. I had moved on from cleaning and was now working as one of the infamous Westminster parking attendants (also known as traffic wardens or parking-enforcement officers) we all loved to hate. The job paid me well, but inside I knew that I would go on to do greater things. In the meantime I could not let any of the people who knew me in Lagos find out what I was doing. I was deeply ashamed of my job because the people I knew looked down on those who did such work, and I cared so much about what others thought of me. If they found out what I was doing, they would start disrespecting and disregarding me, so I kept it very quiet. Only those closest to me knew what I was doing, and even they often made fun of me. They would call me late at night on their way to events in London's West End, wanting to find out where they could legally park their vehicles, and we would all laugh.

While doing this job, I was also the victim of a lot of racial abuse and even death threats. There were days when I would see people cry after I gave them a parking ticket, and passersby would look at me as though I was the wickedest man on earth. This made me feel horrible, and I often went home in a very sad mood. I knew someone had to do the job, but I did not think that person was me, and I began to hate it.

The last straw came on a day when I stupidly found myself on the beat on Bond Street, where I was likely to bump into some of my wealthy friends from Lagos—and I did. At work I always tried to avoid visiting streets that were tourist hot spots. Places like Oxford Street, Regent Street, and Bond Street were risky, so I always hid my face with my hat when I had no choice but to be there. One day a popular girl I knew saw me in uniform, walked up to me with great shock and disbelief on her face, and said, "Toks" What are you doing in this uniform? Please tell me this is not true." I do not remember ever feeling as low and humiliated in my life as I did during that incident, and that was the day I resigned from the job.

I did not see that girl again for a long time, and I suspect she had no idea what effect her comments had on my life. I was irrelevant to her; it was just a passing comment, and then she moved on with her life. But for me her comments were a sharp sword that pierced my pride and made me feel humiliated and ashamed. I made a drastic and foolish decision to resign based solely on the opinion of someone who was neither a family member nor a close friend. Why did I care so much about what she thought?

Jobless though I now was, I was determined to go to university. I completed a university access course in September 2000, and I hoped to start classes later that year.

A Breath of Fresh Air in Neasden

Later that year, something great happened to me for which I am eternally grateful. When I lived in Surulere, Lagos, I had a very good friend who was my neighbor and was also in my year at Kings College. He was now in London to study at the University of Reading, and he'd been living in his family's vacation home, a spacious four-bedroom semidetached house in Neasden. He was about to move into a university residence hall, and the Neasden property would be left empty for months, vulnerable to squatters and theft. His family felt it was better to have someone they knew and trusted living there to take care of the home, so my friend invited me to live there rent free! I was really happy to move there because his family was one of the kindest I had ever known, and I knew I would be OK in their house. Furthermore, prior to this time, I had been praying to God for a solution that would allow me to combine work and university without bearing the burden of rent, fees, and food all on my own shoulders. This seemed like the solution I had been praying for, so I gladly accepted it.

I moved into the house in Neasden that year, completed my access course while working part time as a cashier for William Hill, and gained entry to the University of Hull at the Greenwich School of Management in January 2001, where I studied for a bachelor of science in business management and information technology. It was a three-year degree course that I completed in two years by attending classes during the summer.

A First-Class Graduate

During what counted as my first year at university, I still cared a lot about what others thought of me, and I found myself living the secondary-school life all over again. I was more concerned about my social status than my academics, even though my education was why I was at university to begin with. I hid behind social status because I really did not believe I was intelligent and could get top grades. I had barely made it through secondary school, so a track record of barely average results made me think that was all I was capable of achieving academically. I had strong self-confidence in some other areas of my life, but this did not extend to my education. However, now that I was paying for my education (with some help from my mum), I had a bit more motivation to study, and I was able to complete my first year at university with slightly better results. The good news was that first-year results did not count toward your final degree.

During my second year at university, something happened to me. I was regularly losing peace because something in me said I was heading in the wrong direction and that I needed to take my Christian faith more seriously—that I needed to change my life and stop trying to be this popular guy with the girls. The inner nudge to change was strong, but I resisted it for some time. Then in May 2002, after returning from a nightclub with my best friend, the nudge became so strong that I literally could not sleep. The nudge had taken over my mind, and I could not think of anything else. Thankfully, my best friend was with me that night, so I went to him and asked a few questions along these lines:

- Why are we so interested in all these girls and parties?
- We grew up with Christian values, which are in conflict with our current lifestyle. So what is stopping us from living with the Christian values we learned?

- We both believe in God, so why can't we live for Him? Is there anything more important?

We discussed these questions and more for a few hours, and that very night, my best friend and I gave our lives to Christ and decided to live for Him. Given that we had identified our love of fornication as our biggest obstacle, we knew we would have to make immediate lifestyle changes if we were to have any chance of success. So we did. Now a changed man, I started visiting a local church with my best friend and was no longer interested in nightclubs and events or gatherings that could trigger old lusts. It wasn't as though I felt they were necessarily bad, but I had just made the decision to change my life, and I felt that such gatherings would be unhealthy for me if I was really committed to change.

I started studying the Holy Bible and praying more often, and I discovered the truth that with the help of God, I could do anything I believed I could. I decided to believe in something preposterous: I decided to believe that I, Toks Adebiyi, who was unable to get good grades for most of my education, would go on to graduate with a first-class degree! I found the Bible stories about faith moving mountains so compelling, and I believed in them. What was strange was that my actions followed suit, and since I was no longer interested in or worried about many things, I had a lot more brainpower and time to focus on my education. After that fateful day when my best friend and I decided to live for God, a certain level of peace that I was not used to and could not describe in words appeared within me. In the summer of 2014, I graduated from Hull University with a first-class degree in business management and information technology.

An Entrepreneur Is Born

I started my first business venture with a very close friend while I was still at university. It was a web-based marketing portal for students, with a job board, access to student-insurance services, travel packages, and fashion news. While studying the modules in business management, I discovered I had a strong passion for business. Since I had always admired wealthy businessmen while growing up in Lagos, I was fascinated by the stories of Richard Branson, Bill Gates, Robert Kiyosaki, and Donald Trump. I loved what they had achieved in terms of financial independence and social status. These business gurus seemed so successful, and society seemed to hold them in very high esteem. They also seemed to be living the life by chasing their dreams, and surely, I thought, they must feel very fulfilled.

On the contrary, all the employees I knew hated their jobs and seemed unhappy with their lives. They would always moan and moan about everything, and they looked forward to the weekends like prisoners awaiting release from their cells. Being an employee seemed like a sad life that belonged to the fearful, those who were too scared to chase their dreams and instead clung to the safety and security of a monthly paycheck. In his book *Rich Dad, Poor Dad*, Robert Kiyosaki described it as the "rat race." If I was going to be someone great like Richard Branson, I had to escape the rat race and live a life in which I felt free and fulfilled. I could not carry on as an employee, because my dreams of becoming a great and influential businessman would slowly die.

These were my thoughts, so I became convinced that the only way I could become someone great in life and feel fulfilled was by owning businesses. Thus, with my newfound faith in God, I now felt unstoppable. At church I heard regular sermons about how having faith in God could lead to desired breakthroughs in life. I read many passages in the Bible that made me believe all I had to do was ask and believe, and my dreams would become a reality, so I did.

Despite all my faith, prayers, perseverance, and skills, however, the marketing portal really struggled to take off. I was hardly making any money, and since all the major banks had declined to give me a business loan and I could not secure investors, I had to reinvest and live on the little income the business was making. This was impossible. I got bored with the business and decided to get a full-time job to meet my financial needs while continuing to run the business part time. Eventually, I closed it down and suffered a loss, but my business drive was still alive, and I took comfort in reading about entrepreneurs who had failed several times before making it big.

Aside from dabbling in oil-and-gas trading as a broker for a very short time, the second major business I tried was a property club in which I assisted investors in finding below-market-value property. After the failure of my first business, I was keen to find a venture in which I could make big money in a short period of time, and property seemed to be an area where most successful entrepreneurs had significant interest.

I took a short online course in below-market-value investing, where I learned how to build a business by charging a finder's fee to help wealthy investors find properties at bargain prices. I started trading quickly and was able to build a database of over four hundred investors within a month. I was successfully finding properties below market value and was now being paid several thousand pounds per transaction. This looked like the venture I had been searching for, and I felt I was on track to be the next property tycoon. Many wealthy investors treated me like I was their most trusted adviser, and this gave me a sense of importance, which made me feel great. I had also built up enough cash to start investing in properties myself, so I bought a few. I was becoming a rich man. Unfortunately for me, the joy did not last.

All of a sudden, the world got hit by a global credit crunch that crippled the property market. My clients could no longer get financing to buy properties, and many transactions that were in the pipeline fell through.

Furthermore, several of my own investment properties were occupied by tenants who had just lost their jobs. I found myself in a position where I was paying several mortgages while trying to operate a business that had four employees and was not making money. I tried fighting the downward spiral by attempting to attract international cash-rich buyers who were not dependent on bank loans to buy property. I spent more and more money on advertising to achieve this, but it all proved to be a pointless exercise, as none of the transactions were completed. Eventually, I was forced to let my staff go and to close down the business.

This was one of the lowest points in my life. My girlfriend (now my wife) had had confidence in me, and I'd let her down. I'd let all of my staff down. I'd let my family and friends down. I had no more money and was now amassing huge debt by living off credit cards I could not repay. During this period I wondered where God was and why He had allowed me to fall so hard. It would have been better not to have tasted success, I thought, than to finally taste it and have it stripped away so quickly. I was very sad, but I kept my faith in Him, thinking someday things would turn around. I could not see how they could, though. I had lost all but one investment property, narrowly escaping repossession by successfully defending my case in court.

Milkshakes

At some point when I was drowning deeper and deeper in debt and had nothing to look forward to, my then girlfriend, Abi, decided to treat me to dinner at a nice little milkshake bar and diner in Hampstead, London, to cheer me up. It was winter, yet there was a long line of customers waiting to be served ice-cold milkshakes. We really enjoyed our drinks, and I said to Abi, "Why can't I do something like this? We are in a recession, but food is a commodity that people always buy." She liked the idea and gave me the go-ahead, on the condition that I would have to get a job if it did not work.

I was desperate for anything that could redeem my self-esteem and rebuild my diminishing finances, but where would I find the money to start? I could not get a loan because, after defaulting on credit cards and having some properties repossessed, I now had a negative credit rating. The last thing I had of any value was my car, a Mercedes convertible that I loved so much. I decided to sell the Mercedes to raise funds for the restaurant and bought a very cheap car instead. Now, with a sense of hope and a feeling that God was back on my side and had given me a lifeline, I moved very quickly, discounting fundamental principles of starting a business.

I had only a small amount of cash, and I had to start operating quickly so I could survive. I could not afford to spend time writing a detailed business plan and conducting in-depth market research, so I did the bare minimum. After all, I knew of successful entrepreneurs who had not written business plans or conducted market research. I was overly confident in the product, and I felt nothing could go so wrong that would put me in a worse situation than I was already in. I thought, *What is the worst that could happen? I am already at my lowest.* I was able to agree to a lease and get the restaurant up and running in weeks. It's amazing what you can accomplish when you're under a lot of pressure.

The restaurant was a hit, with many customers patronizing us in the first few weeks. But I quickly noticed how much effort we had to put into generating only a few hundred pounds. This was very different from what I was used to. After all, in my former business, I had been making thousands of pounds on each transaction. Now I had to make several transactions to generate only a few hundred pounds, and the business was management intensive. As a result of starting the business in a hurry, we made too many mistakes, and our inexperience was obvious to our customers. The staff were inadequately trained, so they made many silly mistakes, like bringing a customer a milkshake when he had ordered coffee, arguing with customers, and failing to use equipment properly, which led to unnecessary damage and repair costs.

To make matters worse, I was unable to reinvest the proceeds into the business because I needed money to pay the mortgage on my home. Eventually, the business began to crumble, and no matter what I tried, it did not seem to lead to positive results. I still believed in the business, and I felt the real issue was with the location. There was not enough foot traffic from people who had disposable income. I felt the best thing to do was to relocate to a better location where I was almost guaranteed success, but I had no money for a new venture. Such a dream location would be expensive to rent. It got to a stage where the business could not pay any of its bills, and the utility company disconnected our electricity because of our hefty unpaid bill. This was the end of the business. We could not afford to pay the bill and could not operate without electricity.

Prior to closing down this restaurant, I had been speaking to a friend about opening up a similar restaurant in a busy part of London called King's Cross. He wanted to invest a decent amount of money to generate passive income, and I had found a space in what I felt was the right location, where we could open almost immediately. The existing leaseholder of the premises had a similar-style restaurant but was relocating abroad, so he wanted someone to take over his establishment, rebrand it, and begin trading as soon as possible. The deal involved paying him a large deposit and a set fee every month for the privilege of using his premises and some of his equipment while he maintained the relationship with his landlord. Our lawyer reluctantly drafted a basic sublet agreement. It seemed like a good deal at the time because we were really struggling to find a suitable property in a good location for our budget. The timing of this coincided with the closing of the other restaurant, so I moved all my equipment from the old restaurant to the new one to free up some funds. I tried very hard not to repeat past mistakes, because I had been given a new lifeline. Furthermore, there was now another party involved to whom I was accountable, and he was also a friend I did not want to disappoint.

Despite being located close to one of the busiest train stations in London, we were not as busy as I had hoped. This time there was a steady flow of foot traffic, and I had conducted market research with promising results before going ahead with the property. We had much better staff training and were open late to maximize serving time. We just weren't making enough money to justify the costs, and my friend began asking questions. Even more worrying was that I found out the leaseholder had *not* been paying the rent to the landlord with the funds we had been giving him every month. As part of our contract, we had stipulated terms outlining that the leaseholder had to maintain all rental payments to the landlord on time. We started getting frequent rent-demand visits from the landlord, who was unaware of our agreement with his tenant to sublet the premises. He began threatening us with repossession. A few of the neighboring businesses noticed what was going on, and the owners approached me secretly to advise me about the leaseholder. Apparently, I was not the first to have gone through this. The leaseholder was a con man who regularly structured such deals and duped many people out of their deposits. He had a number of properties that had closed down in the area.

I could not believe the situation I now found myself in. I thought, *Why me?* I was introduced to a number of his previous victims, all of whom advised me to immediately withhold further payments to him until he could assure us that all rent arrears had been paid. I took their advice, and the leaseholder began threatening me when he stopped receiving payments. I tried negotiating with the landlord to see if my company could take over the lease, since the leaseholder was in breach of contract, and he sounded happy with my proposal. However, the leaseholder found out, traveled back to the United Kingdom, and made an agreement with the landlord to clear the arrears.

On one particular morning, I went in to open the restaurant and noticed it was already open and serving. Confused about what was going on, I walked in to find out the leaseholder had taken over the restaurant and was now using my brand. He gave instructions to his staff to prevent my staff and me from entering the premises, since he was the legal occupier of the property. I couldn't believe it; I had basically been kicked out of my restaurant by someone I did not know who was using my brand, much of my equipment, and even my stock! This almost made me resort to violence, but thankfully my girlfriend calmed me down and asked me to return with the police. I informed my friend and business partner of everything that had happened, but I wasn't sure he believed me. The story seemed so ridiculous that I felt a bit silly telling it. I still feel silly even writing about it. My friend traveled to the United Kingdom to see what was going on, and we both went to the property. A fight almost broke out with the staff, and I called the police. The police allowed us to recover all of our equipment from the premises that day, but it would be the end of the business.

During this time my home and other investment properties got repossessed, and my elder sister, who lived with me, and I were displaced. I remember that day as though it were yesterday, when my sister had all her belongings sitting in black bags in the hallway outside our front door. The locks were changed by bailiffs appointed by the court. The tired look on her face and the feeling of helplessness I had that day is something I hope never to go through in life again. I was devastated.

Back to the Nine-to-Five but with a New Approach

Since I had promised Abi that I would return to work if the business failed, I was left with no other option but to get a job. Believe it or not, that was a very tough promise to fulfill, and it took my pastor's counseling for me to go through with it. I am quite stubborn and did not believe in giving up. I had read many books by respected entrepreneurs that said things like "you only fail when you give up" or "when the going gets tough, the tough get going." How could I get a job when I was totally convinced that jobs were for fearful people too cowardly to chase their dreams? I believed no job would make me a rich man, and that was a burning desire in my heart. It seemed right to me to have such a desire for wealth because I felt it was the only way I could be of good use to the church and humanity. However, behind this "help the world" desire was an underlying belief that I had a destiny, and that belief had shaped many of my decisions. I describe this later in the section called "An Inexplicable Encounter."

My pastor noticed this and managed to convince me to think of getting a job not as giving up but as withdrawing for a while to relaunch. I attended a business-consulting training course that a respected member of my church offered me, and I took the professional exams, which I did very well on. Then I dusted off my résumé and reentered the job market. The great thing was that my degree and the business skills I had developed as an entrepreneur were very relevant to my area of business consultancy. They even gave me a competitive advantage over others with more corporate experience. Eventually, I got back into the corporate world as an independent business consultant. I took some comfort in knowing it was a business-to-business relationship and that I was not an employee.

The Property Business Again

After working steadily for some time, I decided to get back into the property business by setting up a real-estate agency and hiring a manager and some staff to run the business while I maintained my job as a consultant. Abi, now my wife, and I had agreed that I would maintain my consultancy while pursuing any business passions as a part-time activity. This way I had her full support to try again.

I structured the business using tips I had learned from *The E-Myth Revisited*, by Michael Gerber, and I worked most evenings and weekends to make my presence felt. Again I tried many things in this business, from spending loads on marketing to investing in an office on the high street, to hiring key staff, but over the years the business proved to be a real roller coaster. We would do well in some months only to see the gains wiped out in subsequent months, and I basically funded the business for years with savings from my consultancy work. This meant we hardly had any savings for a rainy day and could not go on vacations some years. It put a strain on the mood at home, as both of us were constantly working long days and weekends with hardly any rest. Throughout it all I believed I was taking the right approach for our future. I would regularly say, "It is better to suffer today to enjoy tomorrow," and I believed it was the will of God that I should become a business tycoon.

During that period my wife gave birth to our daughter, Eleora, and that was another defining moment in my life. I now had to consider Eleora's well-being with our current lifestyle, and that led to conversations with my wife, soul-searching, and tough decisions. In August 2014 I cut my losses and closed down the real-estate agency, leaving a number of disappointed employees, customers, and suppliers behind. I was mentally beaten and had many questions for God. I was tired of business activities. I had given up.

An Inexplicable Encounter

Many years ago, before my home got repossessed, I had a vision in which I saw myself giving a major speech on a grand stage to a packed audience. I was speaking about how to live a more fulfilling life. I saw it clearly, right down to what I was wearing. This vision was like a dream, except I wasn't sleeping. It came to me when I was driving home from a church service in London. I got to a major roundabout between Mill Hill and Edgware, and for a moment I felt as though I had gone into a trance. The vision felt so real, and when I came back to myself, I couldn't imagine how I had come to the traffic light and was about to take a right turn onto my road, because as far as I was concerned, I was not even in the car!

I loved what I saw in the vision. I loved that I was happy and was making other people happy too, and I looked like someone very successful. At the end of the dream, I'd heard a gentle voice say, "This is who you are going to become, but it is not for you and your family alone; it is also for the good of the church and mankind." When I came back to myself, I thanked God aloud, and as soon as I got home, I told my younger sister what had happened.

Then, about one month later, my elder brother's mother-in-law, who lived in the United States, visited the United Kingdom and stayed with us for a short while. One morning she called me and said, "Toks, while I was praying last night, I felt as though I was getting a message for you. It had to do with you becoming someone great—not only for you and your family but for the good of the church and mankind!"

You cannot imagine my shock when she uttered those words. I had not told her or anyone around her what had happened, and we were not close at all. She did not understand why I was so shocked by what she had said, so I told her about my vision. This vision consumed me, and receiving confirmation of it from a third party made me know it was my destiny. There is something about a dream that you know is linked to your destiny; you just can't stop chasing it no matter what.

I tried to imagine what exactly I could have been teaching on the stage in my dream. I felt it might have been a business seminar, but all I knew for sure was that it had something to do with helping people get the most out of life. That's all I got from it. I also knew I was on a grand stage with some kind of international audience, so I concluded that I had a message that needed to be heard globally. I thought the vision meant I had to become a business tycoon who helped people make money and who was very charitable; after all, I had a strong passion for business and did care a lot for people. My conclusion that the dream was business related became the engine behind why I kept going into business despite all the apparent issues. I felt it was my destiny to be a successful businessman so I could eventually teach people how to become rich. After all, why would anyone listen to me about how to live a fulfilling life if I was not rich myself? That was my mind-set.

I carried on through life with this mind-set, and even after quitting business activities to focus solely on my consultancy work, I still felt unfulfilled and knew something was missing. I was doing well, but I felt like a man on a plane to New York when my intended destination was Bangkok. How had I gotten on this flight, and what could I do to turn the plane around? I became very unsettled and stressed. I was no longer at peace with myself because I now had no idea where my life was heading. I was not used to this feeling of being in no-man's-land without a destination, and it really worried me. I knew I had a dream, but I was not moving in the right direction to achieve it.

Finally, I Found Myself

After becoming a full-time consultant and cutting out all the other business activities that had eaten up all my savings and all my evenings and weekends, I now had more money and more time for myself and my family. Thus, my wife and I decided to live a little by going on vacations more regularly to relax and bond as a family. We could not afford to take regular long-haul vacations to dream destinations such as the Maldives, so we opted for cost-effective but lovely European destinations to which flights were cheap and for staycations in the United Kingdom. We concluded that because we both worked very hard, it was healthier for us to take cheaper but regular vacations rather than infrequent but expensive ones. We even took advantage of a number of promotional vacations during which salespeople tried to sell us time-shares. We got great deals by trawling through websites such as Groupon, Secret Escapes, Travelzoo, and Wowcher in search of bargains and were able to secure a number of amazing deals.

Many of my friends and extended family noticed we were taking four or five vacations a year. They thought I was either making too much money or that I was squandering all my earnings without giving consideration to savings and investments. In truth, my perception of life was gradually changing, and the value I placed on suffering now while storing up wealth to enjoy later was diminishing. I was developing an appreciation for the present in relation to a future I had no certainty I would eventually see. I was now beginning to do everything in moderation. Each month I would pay bills, pay off some debt, save a little, invest a little, and put some money aside for our vacations. I had about five savings accounts, and I named each one. There was Eleora's Savings, Vacation Fund, Parental Upkeep, General Savings, and Stocks and Shares Account, plus my pension.

At the same time that my mind-set was changing, I still had many unanswered questions for God about why I had failed so many times in business if He was with me. I wondered why He had given me a passion for business if I was always going to fail at it, and I also wondered why He had given me that vision. I knew without any doubt that the vision had come from Him, but I did not know what or whom He wanted me to become anymore, and I felt a bit lost. So I made what I now regard as one of my best decisions ever: to rediscover the secrets of life through the Bible.

I decided to study the most important figure in the Bible, Jesus Christ. I believed He was the son of God, so if there was only one person in the Bible to emulate, it had to be Him. I knew if I could just act, think, and behave like Him to the best of my ability, that would be enough to truly live a fulfilling life. So I began studying only Christ in the Bible every day by listening to an audio Bible app called Bible.is. I particularly loved the app because it didn't just read to me; it relayed the events through drama. This really helped me to understand the stories. I took my time, working at a pace of one chapter a day, and would not move on to a new chapter the next day until I understood the current one.

I read all the chapters between Matthew and John and then went back and read them over and over and over. It was not that any of the stories were new to me; after all, I was a leader in the church and attended many sermons, Bible studies, and retreats, and I also regularly read scripture at home. But something was telling me I had to go back to the basics of Christ's teachings. Daily I began learning about life from His teachings and about the true value of material wealth. I started realizing that although I had an understanding of who He was, I did not really know Him.

I had been practicing religion for most of my Christian life with many flawed conclusions that were not in line with His teachings but were rooted in opinions and traditions. For one, I had been chasing wealth so much and for so long, believing it was His will for me to be materially rich. But now I began to realize that out of all the miracles Jesus performed, He did not actually make anyone rich while on earth. Instead, He always gave people what they needed for that moment in time. In fact, the only person who approached Him with a matter that was related to material gain was rebuked, and Jesus told him the parable of the rich fool (see below). The only record of Jesus being angry, even to the point of violence, had to do with people trading for material gain within the temple.

The Parable of the Rich Fool (Luke 12:13–21, New International Version)

Someone in the crowd said to Him, "Teacher, tell my brother to divide the inheritance with me."

Jesus replied, "Man, who appointed me a judge or an arbiter between you?" Then He said to them, "Watch out! Be on your guard against all kinds of greed; life does not consist in an abundance of possessions."

And He told them this parable: "The ground of a certain rich man yielded an abundant harvest. He thought to himself, 'What shall I do? I have no place to store my crops.'

"Then he said, 'This is what I'll do. I will tear down my barns and build bigger ones, and there I will store my surplus grain. And I'll say to myself, "You have plenty of grain laid up for many years. Take life easy; eat, drink, and be merry."'

"But God said to him, 'You fool! This very night your life will be demanded from you. Then who will get what you have prepared for yourself?'

"This is how it will be with whoever stores up things for themselves but is not rich toward God."

I considered the story of the rich fool and discovered that I was the rich fool too because, in that story, the rich fool's only mistake was that he put his trust in his material possessions to secure his future. That was it, and the entire world now knows of him as the rich fool. I asked myself honestly why I wanted wealth so badly, and I realized it was because I wanted to feel important and respected, thereby putting my self-worth and confidence in money. I wanted to say to myself that I had enough saved for a rainy day so I could feel a bit safer about any emergencies that might occur. I wanted to say to myself that Eleora's future was safe because I had invested heavily for her future. I wanted to have the confidence that you get while looking at a bank balance of several million pounds.

This was totally against the teachings of Christ that I so passionately promoted. I had been praying, fasting, and sweating for many years asking for something that was not in line with His will. Why would He give material things that would end up competing with Him as my trusted provider and helper? Would it not be better to correct my thinking before receiving such blessings so I would not get destroyed by them? Money always disappoints those who depend on it. So what was His will, then? Was it for me to be poor? Absolutely not. I studied His teachings and understood that all He wanted was for me to put my faith in Him for my future while asking Him for provision for today. He wanted me to focus on today, and for a great part of my life, I had been suffering today to enjoy tomorrow while on earth.

The only prayer Jesus taught in the Bible was to ask God for one's *daily* bread—not even tomorrow's bread. So why was I so worried about acquiring riches when I had enough for my needs today? One of my motivations was to acquire wealth so I could build churches and help a multitude of needy people to please God, but I learned from His teachings about the widow's mite that He was not moved by those who gave out of their abundance but rather by the one who gave all she had, little though it was. It was enough for me to be generous with what I already had, even if it was not much. The only sufferings Jesus encouraged were those that came from kindness, from sacrificing for others, or for suffering for His sake. And even then the real reward was in heaven, as there was no guarantee that you would live to see a reward on earth.

I learned many lessons from my self-study of Jesus. Another of these was that I had not been loving enough—to myself or others, especially my parents. I was so focused on trying to make a big impact on the world tomorrow that I neglected the little things I could do today. During the period of my intense study of the character of Jesus, my wife and I took Eleora on a vacation to Tenerife. Each evening after putting her to bed, we laid her in the buggy, covered it with a scarf to block out any light, and headed down with her to the hotel restaurant for dinner. On one such night, at the end of a day when I had been worrying about how wrongly I had been living my life and about where I was heading, we were on our way to the restaurant when I heard that gentle voice again. The voice said, "You see how your daughter is sleeping peacefully in the buggy while you are pushing her left and right in it? She has no concern about where she is heading or where you are taking her. All she knows is that Daddy is with her and is in control of the buggy, so wherever Daddy takes her, she knows she will be all right. Why can't you be like that with Me?" That voice struck a chord in my heart. I knew it was God who was speaking to me. That night I made up my mind not to worry about anything ever again and simply trust God that everything would be fine no matter what life threw at me.

My life now is so fulfilling. I cannot really explain it with words, but I feel great joy inside me. I have a great sense of peace, and it is still growing. I am now free from the pursuit of wealth, but now I see the purpose of work as simply to obey God's command and to make society better. My work provides for my family, but I do not depend on it for that provision, because my experience has shown it can fail at any time. It is God who ensures I have constant provision and work, so I commit everything to Him and just trust in Him. Life is so much better this way, and I wonder why I did not discover this many years ago. I now share what I have with my family, friends, community, and society at large. I do invest and save in moderation, but it is only by giving to others that I feel great joy. There are still challenges now and then (mostly self-inflicted), but I can truthfully say everything is great.

Part 2: Focus on Love

Think for a minute about this question: "What do you consider to be the key to living a joyful life?" Is it family, friends, your legacy, wealth, good health? If you selected any of the previous answers, you wouldn't be too far from the truth. However, you probably know of someone with good health who is unhappy or someone with wealth who is unhappy or even someone with a perfect family who still feels unfulfilled and unhappy. The truth is that while these attributes are good and contribute to joyful living, they do not always lead to the desired state of peace and joyfulness when pursued as individual goals.

I know this because I labored hard to build wealth; I kept in shape for good health; and I made every effort to keep my family happy. But still I felt emptiness on the inside that led to a lot of frustration and stress. It felt like something was still missing in me, like I was not doing something I was supposed to do. Thus I felt unfulfilled, and it affected my level of peace and joy. That's because the secret to lasting joy is to learn to give and receive love.

When your focus is on loving everyone around you, including family, neighbors, colleagues, and friends, you will undoubtedly get more love in return. The combination of loving and receiving love leads to lasting joy. I used to think success in life meant having great wealth, a good family, and good health. I now realize that I can have all these and still feel empty, unhappy, and like a failure. I always dreamed of writing a book to help people, but I thought I could only do it when I considered myself successful by material standards. I felt a person needed to be super rich first in order to have any credibility to write a best-selling book. But now my focus is different. I see success as an inner state of mind that positively transforms everything on the outside. The battle is won or lost in your mind. Being truly successful means having lasting peace and joy in your heart and living a balanced life. This cannot be acquired with money but will undoubtedly lead to having more of it, and you will even feel richer than many others who may be financially better off than you.

So what is love? Society defines it many ways—some right, some wrong. People tend to associate love with emotional feelings commonly seen in marriages, relationships, and families. But although these can be the fruits of love, they are not love itself. So, what is love? To love is to give. Love is a state of giving, giving, and more giving. You cannot love people if you do not give to them. Think of love as a verb; it is an act of doing. Those who love by giving but are not great at showing emotions show more love than those who are great at showing emotions but do not love by giving. The greatest lovers are those who do both. There is a hidden mystery or phenomenon on this earth that ensures you receive what you give to others. Those who want joy in life can only get it by giving to others, and giving is how we show love to one another. To live a joyful life, let the act of spreading love (or giving to others) be your top priority, not the pursuit of money or other material things.

Most life coaches would advise people to discover their purpose, write goals, and plan for success. These exercises are very good, and I encourage you to try them. However, there is something even more important than these, something that guarantees you great joy while on earth. It is to love others by giving to them. One of the most commonly quoted scriptures in the Holy Bible is John 3:16: "For God so loved the world that *He gave* His only begotten son, that whosoever believeth in Him should not perish, but have everlasting life" (emphasis mine). This is one verse that really emphasizes the depth of Almighty God's love for humanity—and how did He show it? It was by *giving*! This example is love in perfection, and you should copy it. You can have goals, good plans, and a purpose and still feel like you've failed in life. However, spreading joy to others will always give you a sense of achievement and an inner contentment. Nothing beats putting smiles on the faces of others, and you do not necessarily need structured goals, plans, or even a life purpose to do it. Giving and receiving love is your primary purpose in life. It is a God-given purpose for all mankind. You will discover that whatever your purpose is on earth, it will be linked to this in one way or another.

Read the three short stories below and ask yourself this question: if you had to choose one of these lives to live, which one would it be?

Tade was a man who discovered his purpose early in life: to positively change the world through technology. To achieve this he wrote down clear short-, mid-, and long-term goals. He did everything possible to achieve his goals, at the expense of taking time to show love to friends and family. He invested all his resources in reaching his goals. He knew his purpose involved loving others by creating technology that would make their lives easier, so he focused all his efforts and time on that. He was totally focused on his cause, but he neglected friends, family, and society. He wanted to be a Bill Gates or a Steve Jobs, and he thought he had no time to spare for anyone else if he was going to achieve major technological breakthroughs. Unfortunately, he died before he was able to achieve his purpose. He left many sour relationships because for most of his life, he had ignored those close to him, and he'd become irrelevant to those who mattered most to him. Before he died he was very sad because it seemed like his family did not care about his accomplishments. After his death, his life's work was continued by someone else, and that person finally achieved the technological breakthrough. In the end, little was credited to Tade.

Simi, on the other hand, was a woman who was unclear about what her purpose was in life. She was a bit disorganized and never wrote down any goals or plans. What she knew was that no matter what her ultimate purpose was, it would have a strong element of spreading love to others through giving. She knew it was the right thing to do. Simi spent most of her life and resources sharing what she had with others, and she invested in putting smiles on people's faces. Eventually, she was able to discover her purpose in life, but she died shortly after. She left the world without fully fulfilling her purpose, but she had helped many people get through life. Her community was a better place because of her charitable efforts.

Finally, there was Jane, who was a woman with a clear purpose in mind. Her purpose was to use her cooking abilities to spread love to humanity. She wrote down her goals and had a plan to achieve them. She managed her time well, patiently pursuing her purpose while also taking time to spread love to family, friends, and her community. She started a small cooking business and also volunteered to cook for homeless shelters, family, and friends. Jane was never quite able to grow her business as much as she wanted to, but she was loved by her family and entire community for her selfless acts. She loved running her little business and could afford everything she needed in life. She left the world with great inner contentment because she had worked in line with her purpose and had made her community a better place. She was considered a hero to those who knew her.

In life we all have one unavoidable thing in common: we all die. You do not know when your time will be up. So why spend all your time chasing dreams that you may or may not have time to achieve? Is it not better to live a balanced life in which you are free to chase your dreams and still have time for friends, family, and society? Why not live every day knowing it may be your last and focus on the principal thing—love?

The highest level of love you should aim for is to love others to the same degree as you love yourself by treating them as you want to be treated. If you want others to help you, why not try to help others? If you want business from others, why not try giving others business? If you want others to be nice to you, why not try being nice to others? If you want others to recognize you, why not try recognizing others? If you want others to be friendly to you, why not try being friendly to others? The list goes on.

However, please know that no matter how good-hearted you are, it is extremely difficult—if not impossible—to continue spreading love to others if you do not learn to love yourself. Remember, to love is to give. What do you give to yourself? Do you give yourself things that build you up or things that pull you down? Do you take time out to rest when tired? Do you go on vacation or pamper yourself? Do you invest in your education? Do you eat right and exercise? If you're married, do you spoil your spouse (because, after all, your spouse is part of you)? Anything you do that is detrimental to your body, mind, spirit, or soul is being hateful to yourself. You cannot love others if you do not love yourself.

Which one of these men do you feel is more sincere?

Why does one seem more sincere than the other? Does it have anything to do with the way he presents himself? A man or woman who is stingy with him/herself will undoubtedly be stingy to his/her family and others. A lazy person will undoubtedly end up poor and will be unable to assist people in need. A person who does not exercise, regularly overworks, takes little rest, and is frequently in noisy environments will most likely end up in bad health. Such a person will eventually place negative pressure on his or her family, friends, and society as a whole. This could be considered selfish.

Some other examples of hateful habits include smoking, taking illegal drugs, drunkenness, refusal to learn, bad eating habits, being bad-tempered, pride, and adultery. You must strive to overcome such habits, or they will eventually destroy you. All of us have some of these bad traits in one form or another, and we need to do whatever we can to keep them under control—the most effective way being total avoidance of such temptations.

When you see a glimpse of them around you, run far away from them. For example, if you have resolved to give up smoking and you find yourself in the company of smokers, you should leave immediately. On the other hand, loving yourself is also doing anything that builds up your body, mind, spirit, or soul. Such good habits include getting sufficient rest, pampering yourself periodically, finding quiet time to think, eating fruits and vegetables, keeping calm, exercising, continuously learning, and taking your vitamins. You must love yourself to love others effectively.

Loving yourself is not a one-time activity; it is a way of life.

Loving Others

Once you start learning to love yourself, the next step is to start loving others. However, you don't need to overcome all the habits you know are hateful to you before you start loving others; it is something you should do simultaneously. There needs to be a balance between loving yourself and loving others. Remember, loving yourself and others is not a one-time activity; it is a lifestyle. To proactively show love to others and treat them as you expect to be treated, you should think about the things you wish others would do for you or give to you. If you wish others would be friendlier to you, be friendlier to others. If you want family and friends to call you more, call them more. If you want others to listen to you, listen to others. If you want others to help you, help others. If you want others to be there for you, be there for others. If you want others to attend your events, attend the events of others. The degree of love you give directly correlates to the degree of love you get.

The list of things you can do to spread love is endless, so you get the point. The lesson here is to proactively look out for people you can show love to by doing things you would appreciate if someone did them for you.

Don't get me wrong; I am not saying that you should, say, help someone buy a car because you want one yourself but, rather, that you should help him in his specific need because you would want someone to assist you in yours. It's better to do things for others before they ask you for help. That's when people appreciate it the most, and it shows just how much you care. For example, wouldn't you appreciate it if you were having a party and a friend of yours just randomly dropped off some drinks to show his support, even if he knew you could afford it? It's the little things that count. I remember one Christmas season when I sent little amounts of cash and cards to my family in Lagos. I could not afford to buy gifts for everyone, so

I decided to send Christmas cards with approximately fifty pounds each to contribute to their Christmas lunch. I knew my family did not need it, but I thought it would be better to send something than nothing. I will never forget the sound of my elder brother's voice when he called to say thank you. He sounded so impressed with me, and I know that little act meant a lot to him. I could almost hear his smile over the phone; it made me feel really good. It was a priceless moment.

Early in 2015 I randomly decided to treat my mum in Lagos to a spa day. I wanted to do something nice for her in person, but my options were limited because I was far away. So I called up my sister and sister-in-law, who are in Lagos, to find out the best spas close to where she lives and booked an all-day package that included a massage, facial, hair treatments, manicure, and pedicure. My mum absolutely loved it and blessed me with prayers. This made me feel over the moon. I have since vowed to regularly give a portion of my income to her.

Loving others does not have to be expensive. For example, one of the ways my wife and I regularly show love to friends in my community is to periodically invite them over for dinner followed by televised sporting events or movies. We have found these evenings to be very effective in building relationships, and they are also a source of great joy to us.

You Have Something to Give

What do you have in your hands? What do you have to your advantage: time, skills, infectious smiles, encouraging words, money, other material things?

Do you have one hundred pounds and only need fifty pounds for today? Why not give twenty-five pounds to someone who needs it and invest the other twenty-five pounds? Do you have seven suits? Why not give some of them to people who have no suit? Do you have no money but know an old lady down the street whose garden is growing out of control?

Volunteer to help her with gardening. Do you pray for yourself? Why not pray for someone else? Is there someone at your office today who is downhearted? Give her a big smile, and encourage her with your words. Is there a neighbor you have not seen for some time? Knock on his door today to simply ask if he is OK. You get the message. It's the little things that count.

Do not be discouraged if you are unable to give large sums of money or any other thing. Just give what you can, and be generous about it. Any act of kindness you show to others is like a deposit in a savings account that compounds with interest and someday returns to you in a larger amount. It's the way the world works. The Almighty designed the world that way so that people always reap what they sow in the end. If you are good to others, others will be good to you. If you are bad to others, others will be bad to you. It's a simple law of life, and I challenge you to analyze anyone who has been able to deviate from this rule and achieve the same results.

Generosity does not simply relate to the size of your gift; it is more about giving a bigger portion of what you have. You have no doubt heard about the commitments of Bill Gates and Warren Buffett, who are the richest men in the world, to give almost everything they have to charity. Well, then, it's no surprise that most consider both men to be very generous because they have pledged to give so much of what they have. Furthermore, both have also devoted their lives to charity, giving both cash and time for good causes. You may not be as rich as Bill Gates or Warren Buffett, but you can definitely give as much as they do. There is no difference between the man who gives one pound if that is his all and the man who gives a million pounds if that is his all. The key is they both gave their all.

But shouldn't you have savings and investments for yourself and your family? You most definitely should, but do not consider that portion of cash as your disposable income. Your investments for your family are a good thing and should not be considered yours. You should also invest a portion of your savings and investments for a rainy day with an eye toward giving all in the end if the rainy day does not occur. All other funds should meet your needs and be given to help others meet their needs too.

For those who say, "Well, I need to make money to give money," yes, this is very true. You need to work hard and smart to earn enough so you can give to others, but something inside will let you know when you have reached that level. You do not have to be rich to start giving.

For those who say, "I will keep earning until I die, and then I will give it all away," that is good, but it is even better to make a difference while you are still alive. Warren Buffett used to have the "give it all away when I die" philosophy, but now he acknowledges that a change in approach will make a bigger impact on society. Maybe the idea of giving it all after your death is appealing because you will not be around to keep it. You will be dead, and maybe you only gave it up because you couldn't use it on yourself anymore. It could still be seen as selfish no matter how huge such a gift is. Furthermore, in *The Snowball*, by Alice Schroeder, Warren Buffett rightly describes the most important thing in life as love, and because to love is to give, you should give while you still have life in you. Start today; start now.

Give to Your Parents

Regularly giving to your parents is so important that I feel it deserves a section of its own. There is a great life secret in this that promises great rewards for doing so. In my personal experience, ever since I made the decision to start sending reasonable sums home to my parents, I have not gone without anything. I cannot explain it, but although my income has not increased, I feel much richer. I feel great joy when I hear them say thank you, and although they may not need my gift, I know they really appreciate it.

Compare this to my previous approach, which was to wait until I made it big in life to buy my parents expensive things like cars or a new house. That was a good dream, but there is a chance that I might not live long enough to make that happen. It's much better to start small and start now, and then if you do make it big, you can increase your giving accordingly. Your parents raised you and patiently endured so many sleepless nights and pains to make sure you turned out OK. As a young boy, I suffered from asthma, and I remember how often my mum would stay awake all night, attending to my needs. She sacrificed so much for her five children and was always prepared to give up anything for us, even when she had so little. How can I then turn my back on her now that I have an income? My mum is my hero.

I encourage you to remember your parents in your monthly household budget, because taking good care of them is as important as your own monthly needs. To be clear, by *giving* I mean giving respect, money, time, or any other type of support they will appreciate. To be honest, although many parents are financially better off than their children, I feel I should still show love to them by giving financially if I can afford it. I would advise you to place your parents as a top priority on your list of beneficiaries, and although they may decline your gifts out of concern for you, I encourage you to treat giving to your parents as a compulsory commitment.

PART 2: ACTION POINTS

- Do something nice for yourself this month. What do you enjoy that is good for you? Go for a massage, facial, or makeover; take a vacation or even a short break; allow yourself some time to devote to a favorite hobby; watch a movie; host friends to an evening with tea and Monopoly; visit a zoo or museum. Spoil yourself at least twice this month. Start treating yourself to something every month. I will let you decide on the frequency, but remember, too much of anything becomes bad for you.

- Do something nice for someone else this week. Look for someone in your community or workplace who needs help, and lend him or her a helping hand. Visit someone in prison, volunteer for something good in your community, raise money for charity, listen to someone, or give to someone in need. Henceforth, make it a mission to do something good for someone else each month.

- Give generously to your parents this month. Give them money; treat them to a spa day, a stand-up comedy show or play, or dinner at a nice restaurant; help them pay a bill; hire a maid service to clean their home; mow their lawn. From now on, do something for your parents each month.

Part 3: Guard Your Heart

Do Not Worry; Just Believe

Worry is a silent killer of dreams and a thief of good health, peace, relationships, and everything else that is good in life. If you worry enough about something, it will eventually happen. But if you believe enough in something, eventually it will be realized.

The dictionary defines *worry* as "to torment oneself with or suffer from disturbing thoughts"—the key words being *torment, suffer, thoughts*, and *oneself*. I do not understand why people worry, myself included, because it never produces anything good. You may as well get a good night's sleep so you feel refreshed in the morning to tackle that difficult situation rather than staying up all night worrying about it, only to start your day tired and defeated before you even begin.

Of all the key words in the dictionary's definition of *worry*, the most important is *oneself*. Worrying is a conscious choice you make to suffer by tormenting yourself with thoughts about things you fear. Why would anyone choose to suffer? Why would people decide to hurt themselves in this way? Is it because you think you cannot help it, or is it that you do not know you have the power to choose not to worry? Well, you are actually much stronger than you think, and you do have the power to choose not to worry. I believe worrying is one of the worst things we do to ourselves, and it amazes me how society has become accustomed to this deadly enemy. We seem to have normalized it as though it is a useful habit to cultivate.

People who have the strength to overcome the temptation to worry are sometimes made to feel as though they are heartless or uncaring. For example, in my work as a consultant, I worked on many projects in which almost everything was deemed urgent and needed to be delivered almost immediately. While attempting to fulfill such requirements, everyone would get really worried and stressed for fear that being unable to deliver a client's requirement might lead to termination of their contract. In such environments it was normal to worry, and if you did not panic along with everyone else, people generally responded as though you were not taking the assignment seriously enough. Even though nothing good could come from it, you were almost forced to worry about assignments to show you were taking the job seriously. It is so easy to worry, but it takes great strength to keep the peace in a time of crisis and believe everything will be OK.

I have worried about many things in the past, and from experience I know that it leads to very bad decisions. Another example is when I was so worried about losing a client that I agreed to complete a task in one day that should have taken three weeks. In the end I spent 30 percent of that day worrying about not being able to complete the impossible task and the other 70 percent rushing to produce poor-quality work that caused me more problems than I expected. Had I not worried about losing the client, I would have confidently explained to him what was realistically achievable within his time frame and why I needed more time. I would not have agreed to do the job, and if I had lost the client because of that, it would have been for a good reason. Sometimes it is better to lose a client by declining to rush and produce poor-quality work than to lose a client for producing poor-quality work.

Write this down, and think about it anytime you feel tempted to choose to worry:

> *I choose not to worry about [name your worry]. Worrying will not solve this issue. It will only make me suffer more. Instead, I choose to relax, take appropriate action, and believe everything will be all right in due course.*

Worry is born out of fear, but according to Henrik Edberg, 80 to 90 percent of what you worry about will not actually happen to you. A famous quote from Winston Churchill helps to describe this: "When I look back on all these worries, I remember the story of the old man who said on his deathbed that he had had a lot of trouble in his life, most of which had never happened."

Here are some examples of what people are afraid of that leads to worrying:

- The rich fear poverty.
- The poor fear irrelevance.
- The healthy fear sickness.
- The sick fear death.

Believing Is Also a Choice

During my secondary school (high school) years in Lagos, I hardly got any impressive grades no matter how much I studied. I remember being satisfied and feeling a sense of achievement if I managed to get a C in math and English. I got more and more interested in becoming one of the popular kids and did not consider myself to be particularly bright. The kids in the front row who always got *A*s were from another planet, or so I thought. In addition to being distracted by my desire to be popular, I also had no belief in my ability to reach the top in my academics, and so my thoughts and actions agreed with my belief. As a result, I never achieved top grades during my secondary-school years.

You will eventually end up becoming the person you think you are in your heart. If you think you lack confidence and do nothing about it, you will keep harboring those thoughts until you eventually lack confidence. If you think you are a bad leader and do nothing to improve your performance, those negative feelings will grow, and eventually you will become a bad leader. You are in total control; you can choose to worry or choose to believe. Do not let anything lead you to believe that either worry or belief are uncontrollable. They are your choice to make. Each time worry presents itself, try choosing to believe, and resist all attempts by others to make you conform to the "worrying mentality." You will be a much happier person that way. I can honestly say that since I made a choice to stop worrying about anything, my life has been a lot more joyful. It is a battle I intend to win for the rest of my life.

Mind Your Environment

I read a book by a brilliant investor named Guy Spier in which he explained how he and those he emulates take great care in creating the right environment for their happiness and success. For example, Guy chose to leave Wall Street—where he was a fund manager—to avoid falling into the traps of following the herd or reacting to speculative suggestions. He studied successful investors like Charlie Munger, Warren Buffett, and others and saw how they chose to live and operate in environments that suited their personalities.

Instead of working and living in areas that were popular with the industry, Guy chose to live in a modest part of Zurich. Even though he could afford much more, he chose to stay in an environment that promoted modesty, one where he would not get drawn into the competition of showing off his wealth. He also made sure there were good schools, public amenities, and facilities everyone could enjoy, not only the super rich. He carefully selected an office building that was only ten minutes from his home, and he designed his office so he could take naps and avoid distraction to focus on his priorities.

On the contrary, my story describes how I grew up in a part of Lagos where there was much pressure to be rich. The culture and lifestyle of the rich greatly differed from that of the poor, and many considered themselves second-class citizens because they were not treated equally. The rich enjoyed a great level of exclusivity and could buy their way out of most problems. If there was a line, the rich could cut right to the front, leaving the poor (and a few from the middle class) waiting in the blistering heat. Many such examples created an inferiority complex in people and promoted the love of money and the desire to get rich quickly.

Unless you have lots of strength and think you can withstand all types of pressures and oppression, it is a good idea to remove yourself from environments where there is strong temptation to acquire material possessions. The same goes for anything that leads to any type of covetousness and bad habits. Bad company corrupts good morals (1 Corinthians 15:33). There is a direct correlation between your environment and your level of achievement. The better your environment, the more likely you are to achieve.

While I was at a training course at Harvard Business School, I noticed how much emphasis the institution placed on creating an atmosphere conducive to learning. The campus was more beautiful than any I had been on. It looked like a resort, with many beautiful redbrick buildings and green space everywhere. My room had a view of the Charles River, which was stunning. The atmosphere makes you do your best. It made me want to learn. I remember one of the professors explained how the institution conducted research on whether or not the types of buildings and environment where students learned influenced their performance. Some students took class in one of their newer, uglier buildings, while others took class in the nicer redbrick buildings surrounded by lush greenery. The result was that students in the redbrick buildings performed much better than those in the uglier buildings!

> *Your outlook upon life, your estimate of yourself, your estimate of your value are largely colored by your environment. Your whole career will be modified, shaped, molded by your surroundings, by the character of the people with whom you come in contact every day.*

> —Dr. Orison Swett Marden

Patience Is Quicker Than Impatience

He that can have patience can have what he will.

—Benjamin Franklin

The phrase "patience is quicker than impatience" may appear ironic, but let me explain it with a little story.

The Patient Store Attendant

Once upon a time, there was a lovely man named Timothy who owned a chain of small supermarkets in New York. Timothy was a very successful businessman and philanthropist who was well known for good works in the city. His supermarkets were very successful because he treated his customers with great care and respect. He saw his business as a way of serving the community and not just selling goods. He had a policy in which complaints from all stores were sent directly to him, and he would personally contact any aggrieved customer to apologize and resolve the issue. This level of care built lifelong customers and made his supermarkets famous in New York. Everyone wanted to shop at his stores because staff there really went the extra mile, and each customer was made to feel important.

Unfortunately, Timothy was diagnosed with cancer and given only two months to live. He had no children and wondered what would become of his beloved business when he died. He was concerned others would focus solely on profits and destroy the socially respectful business he had spent most of his life building.

Therefore, he decided the best thing to do was to give the business away to any staff member he identified as going the extra mile for a customer.

Shortly thereafter, Timothy decided to visit one of his supermarkets at random for this test. He disguised himself as a frail, old homeless man and went into the store two minutes before closing time. This was the time when customer care was at its lowest in all stores as staff hurried to close tills, clean up, and restock shelves to get home on time.

While in the store, Timothy spilled milk all over the newly cleaned floor, pretending it was a mistake. The first store attendant who approached him was visibly irritated and said in a moody tone, "Don't worry. I'll clean it up."

Despite repeated announcements that the supermarket had now closed, Timothy took his time and kept shopping. After all, he was a frail old man. A store manager, who was keen to get home, noticed that Timothy's refusal to leave was keeping the cash registers open. The manager approached him angrily and said, "Sir, we are now closed, and I am afraid we can only give you five more minutes to make your way to the cash register."

A very young new staff member, who had only just been trained in the compulsory customer-service program that Timothy himself had designed, saw the frail old man struggling. He dropped what he was doing, approached Timothy, and said, "Sir, what else would you like to purchase today? Let me be your personal shopping assistant. I will help you till you are happy and satisfied with your shopping today. Also, if you do not mind waiting for five minutes after you pay, I can take you home to unload your groceries into your kitchen."

Timothy was so impressed with what he heard that he revealed himself immediately. That very day the young new recruit became the owner and chairman of a multimillion-dollar business simply by being patient and kind to a frail old man.

The store manager and the other attendant both lost out on the opportunity of a lifetime because they could not spare a few minutes to show some care to the old man. Now the young man who had called them "boss" was going to be *their* boss.

How long do you think it took for the store manager to reach his current level in the organization? Probably years. How long did it take for the young man to become the owner? One day. You will undoubtedly get to where you need to be quicker with patience than with impatience.

> *There is no road too long to the man who advances deliberately and without undue haste; there are no honors too distant to the man who prepares himself for them with patience.*

—JEAN DE LA BRUYÈRE, FRENCH PHILOSOPHER

Kill Pride

This might sound strange, but in my experience, poor people can be some of the proudest people, while the wealthy also tend to be quite proud. It takes humility to listen to advice from people who have been there before us. It takes humility to treat others as our equals. It takes humility to love. It takes humility to be accountable to others. It takes humility to receive constructive criticism. It takes humility to exercise restraint.

I will never forget the advice I received from a total stranger while on a family vacation in Bangkok. We were dining at the Peninsula Hotel when I noticed a wealthy-looking man who kept staring at us. He was sitting right next to our table and was dining alone. He stared at us so much that I started wondering what he was thinking. At last he asked me, "Are you a linebacker?" I had no idea what a linebacker was, but I knew it had something to do with American football. I answered politely with a smile, "No, I'm not, but I get similar questions regularly." He said, "You look like a linebacker. I saw you when you were walking around the hotel, and I thought to myself, *this guy is a linebacker*." He then went on to describe his experience with wealthy Chinese men and their fascination with what he considered to be strange foods—such as century eggs, which are eggs preserved in a mixture of clay and other substances for weeks or even months. My wife and I listened and thought he was an interesting fellow, a nice old man. Eventually he said, "You have done very well for yourself. You are staying and dining in arguably the best hotel in Asia." (He didn't know how many times I had checked Groupon and how we had struggled to afford it.) "Tell me," he said, "what do you do?"

"I am what you call in the United States a realtor," I replied. A look of great disappointment and shock came to his face. He obviously could not believe what he had just heard. Then he looked me in the eye and said something that would eventually change my life: "That's a very hard job!"

His words struck a chord within me, and I thought deeply about them. It was at a time when we were really struggling as a business, and I was already questioning the viability of the enterprise. It took humility for me to consider the comment of a stranger instead of being defensive about my business. After all, I did not know the man, so who was he to tell me I had a very hard job? For all he knew I may have been enjoying it, as I believe some others do. But I was not.

I now thank God for that man's comment because it contributed to my decision to search my soul and focus on my priorities. I am much happier today for it. Pride is such a terrible trait; I wish we would all learn to treat it as an enemy. It makes us feel bigger than we are, with thoughts such as these: *Who is he to talk to me that way? I can do it on my own; I don't need you. Without me you are nothing. We are better than they are. You do not belong here. I would rather die than beg.* It really does bring out the ugliness in humanity.

I remember, just before my wedding, my father-in-law asked me where I planned to live, and I stuttered. He was very wealthy, so I assumed he would expect me to buy a new house. But my finances were in such bad shape at the time that I could barely afford to rent a place, much less buy one. Unsatisfied with my decision to continue renting, he offered us money to buy a house. But my pride kicked in. I was tormented by thoughts that my in-laws would disrespect me in my home if they assisted us in buying a place. I imagined scenarios in which I would feel insulted. I was on the verge of rejecting their generous offer when I wisely decided to consult with my big brother, the eldest of all my siblings. He told me, "What is wrong with you? Would you have those thoughts if it were Dad giving you the money? He is your dad now, and the fact that you accept his help does not make you less of a man. Behave yourself, and be thankful to them." Had I not received and accepted that advice, I would have deprived my family of a more comfortable environment, which would have had a negative impact on our quality of life. Today I am grateful to God that I was humble enough to accept my father-in-law's help.

Make no mistake about it: pride leads to terrible decisions, which ultimately lead to a fall. In Proverbs 6:16–19, the Holy Bible lists a proud look as the first of seven things that the Almighty hates. Besides, who can claim to have achieved anything all by himself? Absolutely no one. Everyone owes some kind of credit to someone else for helping him.

Remember these quotes the next time you feel puffed up:

It was pride that changed angels into devils; it is humility that makes men angels.

—Saint Augustine

We learned about gratitude and humility—that so many people had a hand in our success, from the teachers who inspired us to the janitors who kept our school clean…and we were taught to value everyone's contribution and treat everyone with respect.

—Michelle Obama

Be Thankful and Content

Although a majority of people appreciate that thankfulness is a good habit to cultivate, why are so many not content with their lives? Thankfulness and contentment go hand in hand. The answer lies in the myth that extraordinary things lead to extraordinary levels of happiness. In my family, our thing is to go on frequent vacations. This gives us great joy and keeps us motivated in our day-to-day jobs. Without a vacation on the horizon, we sometimes do not function at our best, so we try to book vacations shortly after completing one to keep the momentum going. My family and I go on at least three to four vacations a year. Do you think we are able to go on vacations frequently because we have loads of money? No, we don't. Like most people, we have to budget and plan them carefully. However, we would rather take frequent, affordable luxury vacations than infrequent unaffordable luxury vacations. We hunt for the best deals and mostly buy packages when they are on sale.

For a while when I lived in London, I believed that a good vacation meant we had to travel to dream destinations like the Caribbean Islands, Australia, Thailand, Hawaii, Florida, the Maldives, and so on. Such destinations are much farther away and considerably more expensive for us than European breaks and staycations. I raised the bar so high that it took several months to raise enough cash for any such vacation. We were only able to go on vacation once a year, excluding visits to Nigeria. Of course, this made me very unhappy with my financial status at the time and resulted in me booking more expensive vacations and taking on debt.

It is hard when you cannot afford to do something you love to do. That's when it becomes easy to rely on borrowing to do it. However, now I see things a lot differently. I am thankful for my current status and can afford to go on regular vacations with my wife and young daughter. The strange thing is that I am not spending a lot more than what I used to per year. I discovered that the more thankful you are, the more you mysteriously seem to be in a position to afford even more. I also found out you do not need to travel to exotic destinations to have a great vacation. Some of our best vacations have been within two hours' traveling time, and others have actually been at home! Yes, you read that right: *at home*. We sometimes take time off work to pamper ourselves and relax while still in our own home, and we enjoy it. It is what we can afford to do, and sometimes is better than traveling.

It no longer matters what everybody else is doing; what matters is my need to spend time away with my family at a price I can easily afford. This is my criterion. Do I still get tempted once in a while to spend more than I can afford on vacations? Absolutely! I am human. However, I quickly remember my principle that you do not need to travel to exotic destinations to have a great vacation, and I also remember other affordable vacations I enjoyed more than the exotic ones I have taken in the past. This guides my decisions. Today I continually remind myself and have made it a policy to be thankful and content. It increases my level of peace and significantly contributes to good health. It makes me patient and enables me to stop worrying and believe everything will be all right.

There is a myth that it is only those with little or no ambition who are content with what they have. The truth is there is a thin line between ambition and greed, and many of those who look down on those they see as unambitious are actually greedy. Being content does not equal laziness or lack of ambition. It means:

- You have a balanced focus on enjoying what you have as opposed to fretting over what you do not.
- You are not willing to spend more than you earn, and this will lead to wealth in the long term.
- You recognize that many are less fortunate than you are, so you are thankful because it could be worse.
- You are willing to patiently pursue your goals, and you don't make silly decisions.
- You are not willing to take risks with things you cannot afford to lose.
- You realize that being discontent leads to worry, which then leads to fear. This leads to loss of peace, bad health, and bad decisions.
- You build on what you have.

Make it a habit to be thankful and content with what you have. Your life will be so much more fulfilling and peaceful with this attitude.

He is richest who is content with the least, for content is the wealth of nature.

—Socrates

PART 3: ACTION POINTS

- Consider your environment and everything in it. Truthfully ask yourself if there are better alternatives within reach that would be healthier for you and your family. Take action within one month to make changes to your environment. Stop going to places that bring out your bad habits, and start going to more places that improve your good habits and health.
- As much as you reasonably can, decide today be patient and kind in all you do. It is difficult to show kindness when in a hurry, so take time to be kind to everyone you come into contact with today. If you can succeed with this mind-set for one day, you can succeed for a lifetime.

Part 4: Live Your Life

Be Yourself

Wise words from a wise man: "The people you try the hardest to impress are the ones who do not really matter to your life; those who do, take you as you are" (author unknown).

In any aspect of life—be it spiritual, business, family, or social—trying to keep up with the Joneses is an unachievable goal of being accepted as someone else. It is not possible for people to accept you as someone else; you must be yourself. I have seen many—me included—embark on the endless pursuit of happiness by acting like others only to realize they are a lot unhappier being someone else. It's like a car attempting to drive in the ocean when it was built for the road. Don't get me wrong; it is good to get inspiration and learn from others. But it is not OK to replicate them. You need to be original; you need to find your own path and be yourself. Only then can you begin the journey toward living a joyful life.

A few years ago, I attended a management program at Harvard University. It was a dream come true for me to study a subject I was interested in at an institution I never thought I would be able to attend. Most of the participants were highfliers in society. There were many multimillionaires who owned big businesses, and I think I must have been the youngest participant. I felt intimidated by the caliber of people there, and I was trying to fake it to fit in. I acted like someone I was not in order to make useful contacts who might someday lead me to a life-changing business opportunity. It did not work.

I did make good contacts, but I felt very uncomfortable with trying to fake it. It did not feel natural to me, and I think it even distracted me from making the most of the training and making better contacts that could even have become friends and not just business acquaintances. Instead, I was focused on meeting everybody there to learn about his or her business and add it to my power network. And I think they saw through me. A discerning individual can see through someone who's faking it. Besides, it is much better to have a few quality contacts than a large number of contacts whom you hardly know or trust. It can be difficult to maintain a good relationship with too many contacts and still have that personal touch most quality relationships require. This is one of the reasons why society's elite place far more emphasis on having a few good relationships than on simply amassing a large list of acquaintances they have nothing in common with.

Eventually, I did make a number of contacts, most of whom I no longer speak to. If I could do it again, I would have focused on making the most of the course work, and I would have acted like myself to attract the right people and to build lasting relationships in which there was no pressure to act like someone I wasn't.

It is a wise idea to study yourself to discover your personality, passions, and talents and to learn from those who have been successful (or failed) in similar areas. What you should not do is copy them verbatim. For example, I studied Donald Trump, Robert Kiyosaki, and a few other real-estate gurus when I was trying to make it big in the property industry. I read many books that promoted the idea that by simply copying the business model and lifestyle of the rich, you would achieve what they had. So I did just that. This led to a lot of unhappy moments in my life in which I amassed debt and had many failed projects. But more importantly, I was not truly happy copying them because had I done some soul-searching first, I would have realized that one of my greatest joys in life is to help people live more fulfilling lives. With this in mind as my core foundation, every decision I made would undoubtedly have been different and would have steered me closer to achieving this dream.

The first lesson in your journey toward living a fulfilling life is to be yourself. You are different for a unique reason, and it's OK if many people do not understand you; the people who matter will. Do not deprive yourself and the world of what you have to contribute to humanity, but appreciate your traits and develop them. Let your light shine brightly for the world to see. Being yourself should not, however, prevent you from understanding what great qualities contribute to the success of others. We all need to understand our individual peculiarities and circumstances and adapt whatever has worked for others to our situation. Copying others verbatim is most likely a recipe for disaster. Stay true to who you are. You will feel a lot more joy in your heart this way. You will feel free.

A Great Lesson from Dying Men

In your pursuit of happiness, take time to listen to those who are at the end of their lives. It makes a lot of sense to learn from those who have already lived so that you can discover the secrets of their successes and avoid their failures. Who better to advise you about life than those with experience?

In 2003 a palliative-care nurse called Bronnie Ware did a study of her patients in their last days to find out what their biggest regrets were. Based on her research, the biggest regret dying people have is this: "I wish I'd had the courage to live a life true to myself, not the life others expected of me." I can't help but wonder why these people only realized this at the end of their lives. Could it be that the career of their dreams did not come with the same level of prestige others expected of them? Did the need to feel accepted by others outweigh the need to follow a path they were truly passionate about? Was it the risk of failure they were afraid of? Were they afraid of what people would say if they followed their dreams and failed? Was it the fear of someone saying "I told you so" that held them back? What was it?

Whatever it was that made these people pursue a life that was not designed for them is probably not far from your reason for doing the same. The question is, will you wait till you are on your deathbed before you realize you are making a mistake? Will you generate the courage to start pursuing your dreams, or will you procrastinate till you physically cannot do anything about it anymore? Don't make the same mistakes. While there is life, there is hope. Start today; start now. If you run the race of life on the wrong track, you will undoubtedly struggle to reach a finish line designed for someone else.

Life is too short; it would be a shame to waste it doing what everybody else thinks you should be doing and not what you feel you should be doing. Don't get me wrong: I do believe sometimes a job is a job, and it is possible to be successful in a job you don't love. But to be truly great, you must be passionate about what you do. This is the reason you must evolve from doing a job that's just a job to doing something you love and are passionate about.

Note of caution: It is very risky to take the plunge to solely chase your passions when you have significant responsibilities. It may take a very long time to recover if you fail. Furthermore, those who depend on you may be subjected to unfair suffering. A better approach is to be patient, and get a job or business that provides for your daily needs. Then start putting cash aside, and spend most of your spare time working on the venture you are truly passionate about. It should be one thing only. Keep doing this until you have either saved up enough to focus solely on your passion, or until the activities you are passionate about have grown to a level at which they can realistically sustain your needs. Some people have indeed succeeded by taking the plunge, but many, many more have failed in doing so. I cannot emphasize patience enough; it is really key to living a fulfilling life, and many do not seem to have patience or even want it.

I know it can be difficult doing a job or running a business you are not really interested in, but this is where maturity and strength of character come into the picture. Furthermore, you must consider those who depend on you, like your family, local charities, friends, and even the nation as a whole.

Start now, start small, and do not despise humble beginnings. Remember, chasing your dreams is a way of life and not something you should rush to achieve. However, *you must never stop chasing your dreams*. You only fail when you give up.

Ask yourself: why would anyone who loves and is passionate about cooking, and gets great joy from it, opt to go through life in an engineering or medical job she can barely tolerate? Why would an individual who relishes every opportunity to cook not decide to make a career of it? What are you passionate about? Your passion is closely linked to your purpose in life and helps define it. If you have not yet discovered your purpose in life, you should start searching your soul immediately.

Tip: Your life's purpose is closely linked to activities you enjoy, are passionate about, and cannot do without. You have likely engaged in such activities frequently even if you haven't realized it. People might have spotted this in you and made comments such as "You are a very good listener," "You have quite a big heart," "I think you will be a great artist someday," "You're a natural at…" or "You have a gift in…" Your passion equals the things you love doing.

Study yourself to discover the activities you are most passionate about, and then take steps to begin making a career out of them. This is where you are most likely going to find joy in what you do and make a big impact on society. In discovering my passion, I learned a very helpful exercise while reading *The Success Principles*, by Jack Canfield. It's called "The Life Purpose Exercise," and it goes as follows:

1. List two of your unique personal qualities, such as enthusiasm and creativity.
2. List one or two ways you enjoy expressing those qualities when interacting with others, such as "to support" and "to inspire."

3. Assume the world is perfect right now. What does the world look like? How is everyone interacting with everyone else? What does it feel like? Write your answer as a statement, in present tense, describing the ultimate condition, the perfect world as you see it and feel it. Remember, a perfect world is a fun place to be. Example: *Everyone is freely expressing their own unique talents. Everyone is working in harmony. Everyone is expressing love.*

4. Combine the first three steps into a single statement. Example: *My purpose is to use my creativity and enthusiasm to support and inspire others to freely express their talents in a harmonious and loving way.*

Your time is limited, so don't waste it living someone else's life. Don't be trapped by dogma—which is living with the results of other people's thinking. Don't let the noise of others' opinions drown out your own inner voice. And most importantly, have the courage to follow your heart and intuition. They somehow already know what you truly want to become. Everything else is secondary.

—STEVE JOBS

Be the Best at a Few Things

One of the biggest reasons people fail to achieve anything substantial is simply because they attempt to do too many things at the same time. You only need to be the best at a few things to achieve major success in your business or personal goals. Sound easy? On the contrary, it is actually more difficult to make things simple than to build lots of complexity. It takes a lot of energy to stay focused and avoid the many distractions that regularly come your way. If you are lucky, you may achieve a level of success doing a number of things, but only those who focus go on to achieve extraordinary results. In our competitive world, gone are the days when you could create substandard products and rely on hype to sustain success. In the Internet age, quality matters most in business.

Imagine you were attracted to a restaurant because it looked great on the outside and photos of the meals looked so appetizing that you could almost taste them. So you went inside to try it out only to be seated right next to the toilets, and the waiter took forever to attend to you and take your order. Eventually, you got the meal, and it was nothing special—something you could have made at home with little effort—and to top it off, you got a big bill at the end of the evening. Would you return to the restaurant? Probably not. The hype got you initially, but after trying it out, you concluded that the hype was false. Furthermore, you are likely to advise people not to go there, or—even worse—you could post a negative review on a site like TripAdvisor, reaching an unlimited number of people in an instant. The restaurant would not survive much longer if customers kept having similar experiences.

On the other hand, imagine you decided to try a restaurant with basic decor—nothing flashy but not tacky either. The waiters made you feel welcome and respected, your order was taken promptly, and the meal was absolutely delicious. The price was similar to the mediocre restaurant's. Do you think you would go back? Most probably yes, and you would probably give a recommendation too. Most of the restaurants I frequently visit aren't the ones with hype but the ones that serve the tastiest food in a clean and friendly environment.

A good example is a Chinese restaurant called Wong Kie, located on Wardour Street in the Piccadilly Circus area of the West End, London. The last time I went there, the restaurant was famous for being incredibly rude to customers, yet they were always incredibly busy. Furthermore, customers sat at large tables next to total strangers and didn't have a choice about it. I foolishly tried challenging the seating instructions of the waiter, who hardly spoke English, on my first visit and was scolded for doing so. It went like this:

Waiter (in an aggressive tone): Sit down here.
Me: Can I sit down there instead?
Waiter (in a more aggressive tone, pointing to where I must sit): Not there, here.

It did not help that the friend who had brought me had intentionally not briefed me about what to expect. I was quite upset and reluctantly placed my order. Then the food arrived at the speed of light, and after devouring every grain of rice, I was back the next day and the day after that! I also became a word-of-mouth marketer for the restaurant, telling everyone how great an experience it was and how they must try the food, so a number of my friends visited. Joe Calloway explains in his book *Be the Best at What Matters Most*: "It's not being the best at many things that makes you successful but being the best at the most important things." The most important things tend to be the basics or fundamentals of whatever business you find yourself in. This includes the business of life. That means:

- If you have a donut shop, make the best donuts.
- If you run a hospital, give the best care to your patients.
- If you want a joyful life, be the best at loving others.

Whether in business, socially, or spiritually, our lives are about adding value to others. What is your value proposition? Be the best at it, or nothing else will matter. Calloway explains that you do not need to search for "wow" factors because being the best at the basics is the biggest wow factor you can have.

Gary Keller, the best-selling author of *The One Thing*, goes further, explaining that you only need to focus on one thing to achieve your goals. He says focus on your number-one priority by asking yourself the focusing question: "What's the *one* thing I can do such that by doing it everything else will be easier or unnecessary?" Keller explains that people have a certain amount of willpower each day and that each activity takes up a percentage of it, and "the more you use your mind, the less mind power you have left." He says it is crucial to figure out the most important things and do those first before attempting to do anything else. If the other things don't get done, they don't get done.

For example, here are some great people, in no particular order, who have positively influenced the world. They are known primarily for one thing.

Name	Outstanding Achievement
Usain Bolt	Track and field
Bill Gates	Innovative technology
Warren Buffett	Stock-market investing
Serena Williams	Tennis
Nelson Mandela	Freedom fighter
Malala Yousuf	Promoting child education
Obafemi Awolowo	Political leadership
Jamie Oliver	Cooking
Steve Jobs	Innovative technology
Fela Kuti	Music
Winston Churchill	Political leadership
Michael Jackson	Music
Pele	Soccer
Michael Schumacher	Formula 1 racing
Mohammad Ali	Boxing
Albert Einstein	Physics
Mahatma Gandhi	Peace
Abraham Lincoln	Political leadership
William Shakespeare	Literature

Food, Exercise, and Leisure

Most of us have heard "you are what you eat" many times, but why is it that many of us fill our diets with unhealthy foods? The answer is simply because unhealthy foods often taste better and are easier to get, while healthier foods are more expensive and harder to get, store, and prepare. Plus, they sometimes don't taste as good. The things that slowly kill you tend to be the things that give momentary pleasure.

Furthermore, those of us who try to eat a balanced diet cook most of our vegetables, thereby destroying most or all of the enzymes and other nutrients needed to nourish our bodies. I urge you to read a book called *The Hallelujah Diet*, by George Malkmus, Peter Shockey, and Stowe Shockey. The authors explain with scientific facts why you must not cook your vegetables but eat them raw and how most meats and dairy products slowly kill the body. The book promotes a vegan diet, and although my view is that you can indulge in moderation, you should read the book and make up your mind for yourself. Since reading that book, my entire diet and lifestyle have changed to a much healthier one. I now eat fish and chicken less often and in much smaller portions. On special occasions I may have the odd piece of red meat. I consume most of my vegetables raw, blending them into a smoothie. I've also cut back desserts, which were my vice, to only on weekends and special occasions.

What you eat affects the quality of everything about you. It affects your looks, your health, your concentration, your work, your fitness, your moods, your sexual performance, your finances, and even your breath. It affects everything, including your peace and joy. The healthier the foods you eat, the better quality of life you are likely to have. The trick is to substitute as many meals or snacks as you can with healthy raw vegetables, fruits, and nuts. These should make up at least 60 percent of your diet, and the majority of that 60 percent should be raw vegetables. The other 40 percent of your diet can consist of cooked foods and light snacks low in sugar, salt, and saturated fats.

Be wary of diets that promote a "get slim quick" regime, as you run the risk of putting on a lot more weight when you stop, or worse, you could actually damage your health. A popular example is the protein diet. I know people who have gotten sick and even fainted as a result of putting their bodies through this diet. Your body needs a mixture of proteins, carbohydrates, fats, vitamins, and minerals to function properly, and all should be consumed in moderation; however, some are required in larger quantities than others. There are many useful resources on the Internet that properly describe the recommended daily allowances. If you would like to know more, speak to a reputable nutritionist. They are not too expensive, and I fully recommend them. It would be money well spent on one of the most important things: your health.

Regular exercise, with the goal of being healthy, should also be part of your weekly routine. Although I was previously guilty of it myself, I am now astonished at how many people treat exercise solely as a route to weight loss or to bulk up parts of the body. When this is your only or main goal, you will undoubtedly lose motivation after some time. This is the reason many are members of a local gym but hardly use it. It is the reason many are inconsistent with their exercise schedules. Exercising in moderation is a way of life, and you should plan to do it weekly till you die.

Do you know that if most people treated exercise as an important part of maintaining a healthy lifestyle, instead of a mechanism to lose weight or bulk up, many would cancel their gym memberships in favor of working out at home or in local parks? Don't get me wrong; I am not against using gyms for exercise. But I really prefer health clubs where you can enjoy activities such as tennis, squash, swimming, and golf. When used for the right reasons, gyms and health clubs are indeed very motivating. What you should avoid doing is using them as a "get fit quick" mechanism.

Sometimes I think, *What's it all for, anyway?* After all, you can't take money to the grave. I used to deprive myself and my family of regular vacations and other recreational activities because I really wanted to be rich. I saw recreational activities as a waste of good cash that could be invested. I would save a little and invest a large chunk of cash in my businesses, which eventually went south. Now I do it all, thank God. I take regular vacations, save a little, invest a little, give a little, and spend a little.

The Almighty designed life to be balanced, so too much of anything leads to problems. For example, too much work will damage your health, and too much rest leads to poverty. Some of the poorest people in life are the richest, while some of the richest are actually the poorest. The misguided perception that wealth is strictly financial is flawed on many levels. Ask yourself: why is it that many who are financially rich commit suicide or are diagnosed with depression? It's because riches do not lead to joy; they can only contribute to it.

In the two examples below, whom would you consider wealthy?

John has over one hundred million pounds in his bank account and is on the board of many businesses. He is highly respected as a businessman in society and is married with two children. His children frequently complain they hardly spend time with him because he is too busy. His wife feels neglected and looks to others to fulfill her emotional needs. However, John finds time to attend important social events where the who's who of society are present. John hardly rests or does any exercise but keeps striving harder to reach the top to get more money and power.

John eventually gets to the top but still feels unfulfilled. His children are now older with their own families. They don't speak well of their father and want nothing from him. His wife wants a divorce and has found someone else: he's less well-off, but he will devote his time to her.

Eventually John dies from a heart attack, and his children sell off all his assets. Friends and family soon forget him.

Jack, on the other hand, has one hundred thousand pounds of savings and has built a career around his passion: technology. He is also married with two children, and he quietly does a lot for charity. He is little known in society, but those who do know him speak highly of him. He spends a lot of time with his wife and children, and they absolutely love him. He takes a vacation once every quarter—some short, some long—and can afford everything his family needs. He exercises regularly and tries to get eight hours of sleep each night. He never really achieves greatness financially but is considered great by his family and friends. He feels fulfilled, and his children speak highly of him.

Eventually Jack dies peacefully, and his wife and children consider most of his assets family treasures. If it was important to him, it is important to them. He is not forgotten by friends and family.

In the two scenarios above, who do you think was wealthier? True wealth is a combination of joy, peace, freedom, and good health. You should treat yourself and your household periodically. Have dates on your calendar when you get to do what you love to do. Pay for that massage, take that vacation, go to the theater, take singing lessons, learn a language, and enjoy. Remember, you can't take the money to the grave, so spend a little and enjoy the blessings that are available on earth. It will actually motivate you to work harder and smarter.

PART 4: ACTION POINTS

- Over the next couple of days, truthfully assess your life, and ask yourself whether you are truly happy about the direction your life is going. Why are you on that path? Is it something you consciously decided to embark upon, or are you living life in someone's shadow? Are you living a life others expect of you instead of one that is true to your gifts and passion? Set some goals to patiently start making changes to your life and to align it with your gifts and passion. For example, writing this book is in line with my gifts and passion.

- Take action to start improving your health this week by replacing junk and cooked food with raw vegetables during the working week. For example, you can substitute a healthy kale or spinach smoothie for your regular breakfast. The recipe I enjoy in the morning is 70 percent kale or spinach, cucumber, carrot, Granny Smith apple, and some apple juice and water. You can indulge a bit more over the weekend.

- Think of a sporting activity you would like to participate in such as tennis, golf, swimming, football, baseball, or cricket, and find a local venue where you can regularly participate in it. It can be a health club, park, friend's house, or even at your own home.

Part 5: The Key

Having explored the various aspects of life that can contribute to joy and those that can rob us of it, it is more even important to inform you of the following truth.

I could not possibly say that the things I have discussed are the only things that make life joyful. I have, however, made known to you some of the most important practical lessons from my life's experience in achieving joyfulness. This is also not to say there are no other contributing factors. I must add that, as I mentioned earlier, my faith as a Christian has played a major role in defining my outlook on life and on writing this book.

Your perspective on the role of God is something you will also need to bring on board if the message of this book is to be complete. If you and I agree that there is a supernatural being that fashioned this world and created it, then we also need to build the God factor into how to achieve a joyful life. If you don't believe there is a God somewhere who created the world, I welcome the opportunity to discuss our positions and beliefs through my author profile at www.goodreads.com, where you can ask me questions directly via "Ask the Author," and I will do my best to respond in due course.

If, however, you agree with me that there is a God somewhere, then you should not downplay His role in assisting you in becoming joyful. What God did out of love—which, as described in a previous chapter, brings Him joy—was to give mankind His son, Jesus, so that through Jesus man can find forgiveness of sins, peace, joy, and everlasting life. Being joyful comes from the knowledge that to remain healthy, you must constantly apply the principles described in this book as well as acknowledge your love of and dependence on Christ.

My Prayer for You

Heavenly Father, I pray for all the people who read this book and do not yet know of your peace and love. I ask that you reveal Yourself to them and save them. May they not be misled by the demonization and misrepresentation of religion and the problems it causes around the world. May they not be misled by those who say You do not exist. Father, may they come to know Your peace and love in Christ as I know it. May they understand how much You love them and how much You have done for them by sending Your only begotten Son to die a shameful death for them.

May they understand that You only require belief in your son, Jesus, and their love for You and their neighbors, in return for which they receive Your love, everlasting life, and every good gift. May they realize that You loved them first and are knocking at their door. May they realize that You desire mercy and not sacrifice. Father, help all those who read this book to find your peace and to live fulfilling lives. Father, help them to be and to remain joyful. Amen.

PART 5: ACTION POINTS

- Learn more about Jesus by reading the Bible. Focus initially on the four Gospels from Matthew to John.
- Choose to believe in your heart that Jesus Christ is the Son of God and that He gave His life for you.
- Go to a local church that teaches about Christ, and ask how you can get baptized.
- Live a joyful and fulfilling life, loving God and your neighbors.

Joy is the settled assurance that God is in control of all the details of my life, the quiet confidence that ultimately everything is going to be all right, and the determined choice to praise God in every situation.

—Pastor Rick Warren

Made in the USA
Charleston, SC
12 July 2016